Metal Mystics Take Me!

Anna Donfrancesco

Published 2018 by arima publishing

www.arimapublishing.com

ISBN 978 1 84549 730 9

© Anna Donfrancesco 2018

All rights reserved

This book is copyright. Subject to statutory exception and to provisions of relevant collective licensing agreements, no part of this publication may be reproduced, stored in a retrieval system, or transmitted in any form or by any means, without the prior written permission of the author.

Printed and bound in the United Kingdom

Typeset in Garamond

This book is sold subject to the conditions that it shall not, by way of trade or otherwise, be lent, re-sold, hired out, or otherwise circulated without the publisher's prior consent in any form of binding or cover other than that which it is published and without a similar condition including this condition being imposed on the subsequent purchaser.

Swirl is an imprint of arima publishing.

arima publishing
ASK House, Northgate Avenue
Bury St Edmunds, Suffolk IP32 6BB
t: (+44) 01284 700321

www.arimapublishing.com

What are the chances!
An unexpected musical encounter with the
Melodic Music Band WINTERSUN played on a friends car cd
both inspired and fuelled a special adventure
that took me to a metal music festival in Germany
where I shed old prejudices
and discovered the magic of crowdsurfing
met music heroes Jari Mäenpää, Teemu Mäntysaari,
Jukka Koskinen and Kai Hahtu
Then on to Helsinki in Finland
where I experienced a powerful and unexpected form of Nature
Exchanged my comfort zone for faith and trust
Saw the Northern Lights by a Sacred Lake in Inari
Found my inner artist and poet
Met Indigenous Sami folk
Listened to story telling stones
Found my inner story teller
Saw other worldly visions
Met one of my metal music Heroes
TEEMU MÄNTYSAARI on the Helsinki Metro and
Had a great unforgettable guitar lesson with him
Got into Tuska Music Festival with just my bus pass
Experianced traditional perfect smoked saunas
Enjoyed some wild swimming
Drank clear sweet water in Finland
Visited the Hans Anderson museum in Denmark
Visited Santa Clause at the Arctic Circle
Experienced amazing metal music
And recalibrated my spiritual compass
And then I wrote this journal

METAL MYSTICS TAKE ME

This Book is Dedicated to
JARI MÄENPÄÄ
TEEMU MÄNTYSAARI
KAI HAHTO
JUKKA KOSKINEN
and
ASIM SEARAH
of
WINTERSUN
for the inspirational music

My granddaughters
MORGANA DONFRANCESCO
and
MEGAN DONFRANCESCO
for all your encouragement support and patience

SCOTT DONE
because you shared your love of metal music with me
and cos the CD speakers in your car
go all the way
Miguel for the very first metal story
Natalie Alex Micheal Wolf Vera Martin Andreas
Roman Sarah Lee Patrick Virna Scott
Vlad who was Bnaap
for all your first magic metal stories

Sam Joe Kat
for resonating perfectly
Outi Angel --- for being just that

And Thank you All the Beautiful Folk in the Pics

First there was the Music 11
METAL MYSTICS 15
Mog and Meg 17
Dinkelsbühl 19
SUMMERBREEZE 22
Too Beautiful 29
Crowdsurfing 35
Metal Music 37
Meet an Greet Wintersun 40
Wintersun Gig 42
HELSINKI 44
Soumenlinna 47
Magic Troll Forest 49
Tova Jannssen 51
Roveniemi 52
Arctic Circle 54
Yoonas the Sami Boy 55
Crystal Man 56
Inari 58
Sami Museum 60
Northern Lights 62
Sacred Lake 65
Talk of Metal with Selma 66
Birthday on Haraka 67
Metal Pub 68
Goddess Sketch 70
The Northern Lights 72
Plan B Holiday 73
Ergo at Metal Pub 74
Magic Ateneum 75
Lime Blossom of Soumenlinna 76

Soumenlinna Hostel	79
Speaking of Eluveiti	80
Syncronistic Ware Wolf	82
Ghosts of Soumenlinna	83
Storey Telling Stones of Soumenlinna	85
New Friends	86
Karelia	87
Old Smoked Sauna Cabin	89
Koli Mountain	91
Shakti Dance	93
Stone Sacrifice	94
Magic Stories	96
Story Telling Day	97
Sami Parliment	99
Sami Sacred Island	100
Three Pagan Girls	101
Santa Clause	103
A Leap of Faith	106
Erkel Derkel Elf	107
Painted Goddess Puzzle	108
Great Expectations	109
You Know The Way	110
Majestic Clouds	112
Sami Shaman on the Metro	114
Solstice on Soumenlinna	116
Jerry and the Moika Fish	118
TUSKA	119
Smoke Sauna Tent	120
Amazing Metal Bands	121
Bad Hair Day	122
Chinese Moxibustion ST36	123

Meeting Teemu Mäntysaari on Metro	124
Unforgetable Guitar Lesson with Teemu Mäntysaari	125
Age is just a Number Right?!	128
Vision of the Sea Goddess	129
Outi Angel to the Rescue	130
Floating City to Stockholm	131
Copenhagen	132
Christania	133
Meeting the Elders Odin and Loki	134
Little Mermaid	136
Hans Anderson Museum Odense	137
Vision with the Elders	139
Amsterdam Cannabis Socks	140
Reflection	142
Understanding Metal music	145
Starchild	148
Metal Mystics	151
What and Why Metal Magic	152
Miguels Magic Metal Story	155
Wolf and Vera	156
Collecting Metal Stories	157
Tarde Journeyman	158
SUMMERBREEZE 2017	159
YAAY DINKELSBÜHL	160
Meeting Vlad who was Bnaap	162
Finding Luca and Virna	163
Swimming in the River	164
WINTERSUN at MIDNIGHT GIG	166
Crowdsurfing Love In	167
Pizza Ice Cream and the Rhine	170
Farewell Wolf and Vera	171

The First Metal Music Experiances 172
Honouring the Ancestors 182
The Big Birthday 184
Honouring MOG and MEG 186
In Honour of Wintersun 187

First there was the Music

Music has played a big part in my life from my early childhood where I would listen to popular Italian and classical opera from breakable 78 records played on a small square record player at home.

It was only a few years after World War Two and we did not have very much but some how we managed to have a record player and records.

It was the same record player that I exchanged with a neighbour for three pennies to put in the electric meter when the house went dark and my mother was out working. Fortunately it was returned soon after and so continued to let the music of it work its way into my child's deep eternal memory moment which still has a deep effect on my emotions when I hear it now.

Then when I was nine years old Rock n Roll arrived! Wow what a wake up that was! After years of being sedated by bland croon-y-tunes from the radio.

we suddenly heard music that made you want to sway and dance to the sound of dynamic beats and rhythms, quiet on your own and around strange large exquisite brightly coloured metal and glass beasts that held small records in its metal fingers and were lit up like the lights on the Blackpool seafront.

Then when you put in maybe sixpence the beast's metal hand would release the record of your choice and play it for three whole heavenly minutes and for sure this was the first place I learned to tap my feet in time to the beat and dance like it was the most important thing in my world.

This captivating music monster wasof course The Jukebox and it quickly arrived in most cafés and arcades all over England ensuring the birth of a new trend of spontaneous dancing in public places from both teenage girls and boys

This as 9 years after World War 2 was no small event.

Dancing boys could be Teddyboys, dressed superbly in three piece suits with soft soled blue suede shoes and very groomed hair or blue jeaned motorbike boys wearing leather jackets and very styled greased hair wearing long black leather tapered shoes called Winkle Pickers.

The girls could have many petticoats under a very wide colourful skirt that could sway and carousel in harmony with their dancing or tight as you like knee length skirts.

This restricted the girls leg movements so much as to allow only the taking of minimum tiny steps and with the addition of stileto high heels brought every hip movement fully into focus as the girls wobbled delicatly along the street to the tune of their metal heels klick klacking.(This in my generation was the symbol of the ideal feminine girl.)

When I was twelve I would go to the live rock n roll dance band playing in the old ballroom on our seaside pier and dance with someone else which could be a girlfriend and if lucky enough would be asked to dance with an actual boy.

This new music was both a revolution and an evolution to my generation as it musically challenged the status quo and heralded a new cultural conciousness, as it left many futuristic doors open in its wake which I wholeheartedly embraced including 3inch high heeled shoes and clothes to match.

But musical fashions were changing fast now for me so at the ripe old age of 13 when folk music had become popular there was a 50s beatnik revival which was far more of an introspective philosophy, but it resonated with my melancholic nature so I swapped my heels for green suede ankle boots 501 blue hemp levi jeans and blue/white striped long sleeve t-shirt.

I haunted folk clubs and sat in our local coffee bar which I thought was really hip cos the walls were decorated in cool Hessian sacks and we conversed in more serious melancholic tones now, about what? religion? our own beliefs? Yes all of that I am sure spoken albeit from a very youthful and naïve but quiet intense perspective.

But we never discussed the 1939/45 war as there was an unspoken taboo about talking of the recent war in England and so I never heard about it at school and rarely got mention of it from an older persons experience and certainly not from my mother whom I discovered many years later struggled with being an Italian in England and my father was in a prison of war camp on the Isle of Man. (which actually was not too bad)

But this war that had effected every aspect of life for about six years was never my generations topic of conversation and so when an occasional embittered remark was made by an old veteran who had fought in it and was offended by our youthful pranks we had no understanding and we just felt separated from the older generation and all past events and it is only later I asked older folk about their experiences at that time as there was much bravery and sacrifice which I feel does need honouring.

METAL MYSTICS TAKE ME

I also wanted to enjoy classical music but was ridiculed at school for it so kept that a secret until I was fifteen and left home and with my first wages I bought a record of Beethoven's Moonlight Sonata.

Trad Jazz was now popular and strangely could be danced to and it was fun!

Then folk music got very serious with the arrival of Bob Dylan whose songs became a beacon for my new socially aware young generation, which was the way that my generation seemed to want to go and at age fifteen he was a hero for me for some time. I remember later at 16 paying seven shillings and six pence to see him playing acoustic guitar live at the Albert Hall in London.

Rhythm and Blues and straight blues was happening for me now and I did like it a lot with all the folk clubs in london fully embracing the new folk style.

The Beatles had arrived when I was 15 and at art school where they quickly gathered a great following of screaming girl fans.

But some how that music passed me by as I was still into folk music and being melancholic but I could not ignore the exciting change it brought complete with new hair styles and clothes.

I have to make mention of Leonard Cohen as he arrived in the late sixties and I was playing and singing his songs on guitar with my talented son years later.

When I was eighteen I followed many of my generation and went on a spiritual quest to India. (A war at the time prevented me from crossing the closed border with Pakistan and so that dream had to wait)

I hitch hiked through Turkey, Persia and Afghanistan to a tea shop in Baluchistan, Pakistan where I had the opportunity to hear a simple stringed musical instrument played to a song in Urdu that fascinated me even though I did not understand the words but no records were yet available to me of folk music from other cultures till about a year later when the Indian Sitar music arrived in record form and I recall that George Harrison of Beetle fame learned to play one after his spiritual trip to India.

When I was nineteen I continued my generation's quest for spiritual enlightenment which was supported by psychedelic visionary music and then more lastingly by a music that I don't think was given a name.

I think I just called it visionary hippie music and years later I was still listening and playing the music of The Moody Blues to my granddaughters as I felt they mirrored the heart and spirit for my generation which incidentally is Leo in Pluto with lots of Dreamy Neptune and we used all that force to banish all signs of ageing both inner and outer.

Cos when you've been Streaming down the Skyway on your Cosmic Wheels (Thank you Donovan) then the idea of Walking down the Highway in your Boots of Steel and knitted woollen twin set and slippers just is not an option.

Punk music? The antithesis of everything my generation believed in so quiet challenging. Disco was fun for a while and New Romantics ok Trance? Hmm!I heard it playing a lot when l was recently in Anjuna Goa. Wrap Hip Hop mix? I liked sometimes.

Pink Floyd? TIMELESS and love it now still especially CRAZY DIAMOND.

METAL MYSTICS

Time passed then to 2013.

I was in Scott's car he's a young friend of mine who likes music a lot and he put on a CD in the player.

The music began with a sweet melody and then suddenly just 'Took Off' in an explosion of sound colour and absolute passion.

It was as if the very gates of Asgard had opened and unleashed some phenomenal elemental force into my head and it cascaded into all the cells of my being and shook my whole body. "Wow! Turn it up" I gasped!

My friend Scott did so as we continued our long journey.

This new musical experience was transporting me into a magic dimension and I did not want to leave. "Play it again" I urged when it had finished and my friend again obliged.

It was a long journey and I refused to hear any other sounds except the one playing that was by now really enchanting my world and changing it forever and there was not a thing I could do about it nor did I want to because this new music stuff was setting my soul on fire and inspiring multidimensional visions!

Later I asked for the name of the group "Wintersun" was the reply, "From Finland". Album name was Time I.

Later I bought the CD and studied it and now I could see what the musicians looked like and they did not disappoint for all four of them were very handsome with a definite Nordic look "So these are my Nordic Metal Music Gods" I thought to myself.

I now could look at and read the words of the songs which playing full power in the car CD player was difficult to hear the words well and I was enthralled by them now.

The songs were about things that I have never heard from a music band before.

Like Time falling away and Dimensional Doorways.

And it was like all the singers became the very Force of Nature itself and gave it a voice to melodically relate the absolute Elemental beauty of Stars Snow and Dark Winters with such an eloquence and passion that I had not heard before.

Time I began like a sweet Japanese meditation music indeed I could do Tai Chi to it which would not be out of place.

Then it gradually changed in mood till it reached meteoric operatic level and after effortlessly gliding back to Melodic Tones

All beautifully executed with a mixture of exquisite growls to full operatic tones then melancholy tones and all to an atmosphere of passion played with perfect music. And as I relived the first impact of hearing this Time I, I knew that I was now taken into an Ancient Realm all set in a snow filled landscape where Visions of an Ancient Goddess and Warriors were common place and not only Visions but Poetry for that time was truly awakening inside me.

And I also knew that this landscape felt Sacred and was intricately entwined with this new music of Wintersun band which would fuel my journey to find a new Spiritual form of expression.

I bought the 2nd CD also which was separate songs and was titled Wintersun and I enjoyed the diversity of each separate song on this one and between listening to the two my musical life was complete.I did not know what the Visions of Goddess and Ancient Warriors were about yet but l felt a need now to travel to the land of the Midnight Sun to find the meaning for the visions and poetry and I also wanted to experience a live contact with my musical heroes who had sparked this new expression of spirituality.

And so with the help of my granddaughters Morgana and Megan looked on line till we found a music festival where Wintersun were playing.

Mog and Meg

Summerbreeze Festival Dinkelsbühl in Germany was not quiet Finland but I had to follow the music of my band and the Visions.

So Morgana and Megan booked a ticket for me on line for August.

An air flight proved too expensive so we booked a coach to the nearest point of destination and as I really wanted to visit Finland l booked a direct flight there for two days after returning from Germany.

It would be a good place now to mention the style of my new musical romance because as I have now lain down how I feel for it there must be no doubt or misunderstanding about it being a spiritual experience and also the advise that Meg is about to give me would not make sense otherwise.

My musical band Wintersun play Melodic Death Metal.

"Nanna stay away from the Mosh pit" said my Megi in a worried tone.

She'd heard that a Mosh pit is a place of unpredictable wild dancing at Metal Music Festivals and she was concerned for my safety!

I was touched by her words cos it's usually me who does the worrying and I promised to stay away.

I was so grateful for the help of my granddaughters with the on line bookings, and not least for their acceptance for my new spiritual path into the most controversial music style and their patience for my rather juvenile enthusiasm for my new Melodic Death Metal band Wintersun.

Buying tickets on line was a new thing for me cos in the olden days of rock n roll and folk we turned up at the gig venue and buy the ticket so many reasons to feel grateful for Mog and Megs help without it this adventure would not begin.

The day arrived and I caught the coach to Germany.

I was fortunate to sit next to a sweet young Polish man and he liked metal music also Peter was his name and we had interesting conversations and at a motorway stop place I saw three Service Berry trees growing in the courtyard and I was amazed as this tree is so rare and it is incidentally the first berry I gather when foraging in the UK time was short with five minutes only but

I picked just a few. Then I got a surprise birthday call from Peter and metal music CDs as a gift and I wish I could thank him but I didn't have his mobile number.

Travelling to Dinkelsbühl from Stuttgart was quiet simple and Meg had sorted me out with a camp site on line which I was most impressed with.

Dinkelsbühl

So I found it easily and booked in and began to set up the small borrowed tent only to discover that, try as I may, setting up a simple tent was not one of my better known life skills. Help arrived though and I settled in. The camp site was well organised into tiers and lines of caravans where neat rows of flowers were growing in and around them.

There were really great shower blocks and I was camped by a small lake with ducks in where swimming was popular with the many German families and I was able to swim and sooth all the travel stiffness.

But it rained quiet a lot and I had booked five days there and my borrowed tent leaked and the sleep mat I borrowed disintegrated so there was room for a philosophical attitude if I chose to adopt it which I did do momentarily each day but being sleep deprived did not encourage it.

I met Wolf and Veronica a handsome German couple who were also on their way to the Metal Festival and they befriended me then generously spent time introducing me to other metal music.

Wolf was amused that l had brought camping food from the UK "Do you think it is after the war when food was scarce" he asked. I saw his point after shopping in the town as food was cheap and good.

The town itself was a tourist attraction with very old big character houses and a Faery Tale castle in a lake with many charming cafés and lots of Japanese tourists

I met Virna and Luca, a very attractive couple at the camp site from Italy who were also going to the Metal Festival. Virna was dressed appropriately in denim waistcoat with an Iron Maiden design on the back and interesting boots.

"We are known as the Aunties" she said as we look after the young folk who party outside the festival gates all night long before it opens.

"We are family" Virna said.

I mulled over this new info about metal music family idea and then we all met Bnaapp from Ukraine (his name obviously was much longer and spoken with a speed that left me so confounded and embarresed at not understanding it that l chose what sounded like a short version) He had very long brown hair and was on a motorbike with leather gear that reminded me of medieval armour and that evening we all walked to town and sat in a café with a big copper beer making vessel and there we met another Italian couple, good looking Vincent and Serena and we all drank excellent German beer and passed a pleasant evening.

METAL MYSTICS TAKE ME

SUMMERBREEZE

Dinkelsbühl proudly proclaims that every year they are happy to play host to thousands of metal fans who attend the Summerbreeze festival and it was charming to see hundreds of metal fans in that setting.

I didn't know it at the time but it would become a morning refuge from the rain.

Wolf and Veronica gave me a lift to the festival and I set up tent next to their camper van after signing in and having an Id bracelet.

And as it turned out I would be very relieved for the comfort of their friendship and hospitality as it rained I think every day and so their invitation for me to sit in with them saved me from a rather damp tent and as such the camper van became a refuge from the weather.

The festival site was in a large grassland area of the country side split into two parts one for the stage area and the other for the camping.

These two worlds were separated by a security gate split into about five narrow entry paths with each one manned by a security person and out of all the folk that I met there the security gave me most hassle for their disrespectful attitude and rough handling.

They rifled through your bags as if you were a villain and I had daily verbal exchanges with them where the F word was liberally used by myself to express my feelings for their behaviour.

I remember now that maybe ten to fifteen years past I'd heard that there was a new kind of security guard that was three parts thug and as this was at my old festival haunt of Glastonbury festival so I was outraged.

There were two big main stages which were placed side by side to each other as they took turns to play so in that way nothing was missed and then one very large marquee for not so A-list bands and then two small stages on the main drag showcasing new bands.

There was a large outdoor café area with benches and tables and much beer stands all around.

In the market area I found Virna trying on some new clothes and she was in full festival mood she and Luca work very hard in Italy to save for this festival and I enjoyed to see her having a good time. I wondered around with her to the market stalls where there were all the fashionable clothes for metal maidens eg black and red long lace dresses with black bodices and the most amazing boots trimmed exotically with silver metal which I took a few photos of.

I began to get the connection between this metal music and ancient warriors, as I saw many cattle horns on sale as drinking vessels and then there was some young men wearing red ancient warrior kilts and as the ancient ways was my fascination I was noticing whenever it revealed itself and I was fast shedding a lot of preconceived ideas about metal fans as every man and boy I came across were really delightfully friendly and I noticed that the drunker they were then the more loving they became. Indeed the loving atmosphere would rival that of Glastonbury festival, where three generations of my family enjoyed three days of great music theatre and children's area.

And I found myself thinking almost out loud "So this is where the Hippies went to."

This whole Metal music festival was an exciting assault on all my senses from the smell of festival food the sight of many beautiful smiley folk with extraordinary tattoos and interesting clothes to the many different sounds of singing and music.

I had asked a group of young men to recommend a good metal band because to date the only band I knew were Wintersun and I felt that I needed to hear much more of this new music as I wanted to avoid becoming too obsessed with my one albeit amazing band.

"Eluvieti" was given as the name and so I found the place and time of their gig and arrived at a main stage and it was clear to see their popularity as there was a big crowd around me that grew right to the main stage.

So I remembered Megs advise and stood way back outside of all of the audience and I decided to film a bit and take pictures from a position I'd found standing on a metal seat that served also as a barrier.

I soon realised there were three (older than teenagers) friendly men standing behind me in protective mode and I thought that was cool and it felt quiet natural as this was my first ever live metal music festival and I was full of excitement of the expectation of a totally new experience and the men just felt part of the event.

The stage was big and square and on either side there were huge screens to watch the bands playing comfortably from a distance. (just like Glastonbury really)

Eluvieti had already begun to play and clearly they were really popular and I got a sense from seeing the lead singer on a screen that he was a master of his musical instrument.

METAL MYSTICS TAKE ME

Too Beautiful

Suddenly some thing really unexpected happened that just blew me away.

I saw a smiley young woman and man gently lifted above the crowd and carefully carried from up stretched hands to hands toward the direction of the main stage.

My reaction to this phenomenon was immediate and very emotional and I just stood there with one arm raised holding a camera as I sobbed uncontrollably.

"But why the tears there?" Ill tell you why, "It's all too beautiful"

These are the words of a song from the Small Faces called Itchycoo Park that I do love even now and it mirrors my feelings from that experience which I do note as my first magical experience on this journey.

So I also had a dilemma now cos I realised that I could not film and sob at the same time and as I did not want to miss a moment of the magic.

I decided to reign in the tears and that done I then took lots of pics of folk being gently lifted and carefully surfed from one set of raised hands to another.

The destination was the front of the stage where the surfers were gently collected by the trained security guards and placed on the ground.

I knew the name of this event as I d seen it a little on tv before but it did not prepare me for the emotional reaction to seeing it live.

Something about it really got to me and at the time if you d asked me why then I would not have been able to answer.

It just stirred something very deep inside of me on a purely emotional level that was so powerful it broke through all my mental barriers of social behaviour.

And the tears had their day.

But it was the most amazing thing I had ever seen in a crowd of young folk.

And in that one instant I transformed from being an outsider and tourist to feeling a part of this awesome event and I took pics of all the smiley young folk that were Going Up, and what's the name of this incredible event?

It is called Crowd surfing and to see and film it made me feel really happy.

METAL MYSTICS TAKE ME

METAL MYSTICS TAKE ME

CROWDSURFING

A while later two boys who had seen me filming invited me to Go Up! I said a "No" followed quickly by a "Yes please" and then l was Up and holding on to my camera to try and take pictures of the crowd and gently surfed to the front of the stage (feeling a bit like a long caterpillar) where l was gently gathered up by a security guard and placed on the ground and it was really great fun to do and I just felt safe and enjoyed the soft landing in the arms of a gentle security guard.

I did not consider any thoughts of danger about being crowd surfed.

I think that I was just being in the moment and I wanted to show gratitude to the two lovely boys who were kind enough to honour my sense of fascination and commitment to the event by offering to safely Take me Up. (Awesome Babes)

The next day l found Vincent who looked very handsome in a pirate's hat and long coat and Serena and told them of my adventure l asked them to film me going up again for my family! and it was agreed that Vincent help me up whilst Serena filmed the event.

Vincent took my hand firmly and lead me around for quiet a while till we came to two men and he spoke to them in another language then left me with them and l was Up! Primal Fear are a metal band that were playing and singing something about Jumping into the Fire as I crowd surfed which I thought was quiet appropriate.

It was again a truly exciting experience that I surrendered to with my arms outstretched and body in relax mode wearing pink and green wellies on my feet.

And when I told my son Mathew about it he said he was proud of me! Which surprised me a little but also pleased me a lot.

Then much later when I was back home I looked at the video on my computer and after the third look I saw that one pair of hands never let me go! I laughed and nearly cried as I was so deeply moved by that cos I guessed that Vincent would have told these guys not to let go which I thought was a really brotherly act.

Metal Music

After the crowd surfing event I began to notice the body language of the audience more and many hands were raised up and the two middle fingers were closed whilst the index and pinkie finger were straight as if in a salute and then firmly waved in response to the band on stage playing and this is a universal classic metal music sign apparently.

The audience also showed their delight for the band chanting Hey! which reminded me of warrior calls and then some men would shake their head back and forth in time to the music and this is commonly known as Head Banging and some guys with beautiful long hair would roll their head around allowing it to wave like a flag.

Indeed even the metal musicians were doing the same with varying lengths of hair sailing above and around their good looking faces.

And that's the metal body language sorted to date.

As this was my first contact with live metal music the music and words were clearer for my ears and I could hear now the different expressions of metal music sound and being able to distinguish Heavy metal from Folk metal and Fantasy metal and my favourite band Melodic Death Metal of Wintersun. After visiting a few bands I was able to hear the different subjects sung about now most of which are taboo in mainstream pop music like extreme pain fear, dying, freedom, death, rebirth, immortality of the soul, rage, hate, religion and Paganism and all magnificently and passionately sung and growled and shrieked and screamed whilst played on beautiful electric guitars and other musical instruments to all kinds of complex styles whilst at the same time all sharing a passionate delivery theme.

Indeed I have never experienced so much passion on a music stage before.

I noticed that the angry growls and words and thrash guitar music did not whip up an angry response for the listener, on the contrary it looked as if the audience was ecstatic as if the strong emotions were lifted through this medium of music and I was catching impressions now of the scene where by the band would possibly represent a tribal Shaman that gathers a deep strong emotions from the hidden depth of the collective unconscious and mirror it to the listener through music and song and in this way it helps to transform negative energies and demons. Heady Stuff! I was fascinated by that thought.

I shed the last remnants of old prejudices for metal musicians that day at a Meet and Greet with a band unknown to me who were so gentle and friendly with no ego problems as it totally disarmed me and left me quiet speechless.

Then seeing some heavy metal bands because the lyrics were certainly informed and eloquent and the whole Summerbreeze experience put into perspective about the aggressive reputation of metal bands in my mind and raised my understanding, cos I saw that some of the bands may have strange painted faces that make them look dark or aggressive or just strange but they are not aggressive or dark and they will be all kinds of friendly if you talk to them and I realized they are just painting a picture of an aspect of a subject just as any good actor would do and when they do play the song it is delivered with that same courage and passion with every different style played like.

Melodic Death Metal, Power Metal, Fantasy Metal, Folk Metal, Pagan Metal, Black Metal, Heavy Metal, Death Metal, Doom Metal, and Thrash Metal.

I don't want anyone to think that I want them all to love metal music cos that just won't happen as musical taste is a very personal thing and cannot be forced and most of my family don't listen to it and of course I'm cool with that but I do tolerate listening to jazz as my Little Lad Mathew likes to play it at home.

Wintersun have a song about death and rebirth it is called Death and the Healing which is of course played melodically and superbly.

> A snowstorm blew inside a wolf's eyes and the frozen tears covered all the mountain sides.
>
> But then the time got by and the wolf died and someday that wolf would be I
>
> Time is the Death and the Healing Take your last breath cos death is deceiving
>
> Time is the past now and tomorrow Days fly so fast and it leaves me so hollow.
>
> That's not all the words but it can be found on YouTube.

Meanwhile at Summerbreeze it rained every day and I was sleep deprived when my group Wintersun appeared at the place where you can get their autograph and I need to relate that my generation were too cool to scream at our music bands and I certainly never have been a screamer but I did feel really the enormity of the experience of meeting with my music heroes.

Meet an Greet Wintersun

I had queued for two hours for this meet and greet holding tightly to the two CD lyric booklets to be signed when I saw Jari Mäenpää and Wintersun.

He has a very tall and comely Viking look with blonde hair blue eyes and a soft clear handsome face and then they arrived and I was first in the really long queue.

I told him I would travel around his land but even for that very short time of close eye contact it was clear his energy was really special and I would say quiet Crystal orientated as auras go and his face had a clear soft beauty which appealed to my artistic eye and even though I was so sleep deprived and felt and probably looked like a swamp creature I was aware that I was gazing into the eyes of a living legend and yes it was a truly Awesome event even for a Swamp Creature.

I had taken with me a magic story book that I d created with my grandchildren and as my wonder group Wintersun had given me their very best I wanted to give them my very best back which was my creative art and so l gave this book to Teemu Mäntysaari as he was the first one l made contact with close up as possible as they were really high upon a secured closed in stage and I was on tiptoe but I could see he had truly a beautiful young warriors face with dark hair and eyes.

Then moving swiftly on there was Jukka the handsome base guitar player and I caught on camera a warm smile as he talked with another fan then Kai the good looking drum player was smiling also engaging with another fan.

I was aware that I was a new fan so I was not so confident to engage in conversation and this meeting was brief as there was a time limit and many fans needing to have an autograph so I just stepped back and took some pictures. Jari is a man of many faces and I am glad I caught a soft side on camera and then two more hours they were on stage.

I'd missed getting a front stage spot so asked some fans there if I could stay and film setting up and this wish was granted and then after I was back at a corner side in front of a speaker with small camera raised and ready to film.

Wintersun Gig

Wintersun arrived on stage to young fans gently chanting their name and waving their hands to the beginning music of the gig which was Time I.

The stage was awash with many lights pouring down and weaving in differant directions changing from white to blues purples and greens with many colours melting in to each other and this was the landscape that the beloved Wintersun band arrived at.

This is a sight I will always remember as the love and devotion for their band shone out like a beacon throughout all their gentle hand waving whilst chanting the name Wintersun and it was all the more noticeable as it was in complete contrast to previous gigs of the other bands playing at the festival where the fans were more energetic in their display of devotion.

And this chanting of Wintersun's name sounded more like a devotional prayer that sounded so gentle that l could feel it in my heart and I was deeply moved by it to wittness and realise the depth of feeling that Wintersun inspires from their fans.

The music of this gig began like a delicate Japanese meditation sound and then it suddenly Took Off.

I recalled with joy the first time I heard it as it became a delicious combination of purry growls to an exquisite high tenor voice from Jari Mäenpää and the harmony from the band.

The words of the song wove a story of Other Worldly Elemental Forces of Nature and of course the music was magnificent.

But a security guard was constantly in my way collecting the many crowd surfing fans and I was yelling and cursing with sheer frustration.

It was months before I could bear to look at the footage cos I was sure the sound of my curses would dominate the video but when I did eventually look the sound was so warped because of being in front of a speaker that it was that bad as I was positioned in front of a giant speaker and so most of the sound was warped but I could hear clearly the uttered curses. Uurgh!

So that was the first chapter of the adventure but l did not have time to reflect on it as l now had just two days to prepare to fly to Finland where Megi had booked an Airbnb.

The flight was a challenge initially as l was coping with a phobia of flying but being determined thus far to fulfil a dream l pretended to be a dragon flying with other dragons and in this way l was able not only to survive the flight but also enjoy it.

HELSINKI

I arrived in Helsinki airport at lunchtime, caught a city bus and was there in one hour and it was not what I had expected as in my mind it was much more of an old fashioned place with perhaps some dirt roads! Hmm!

This would not be the last time my expectations were challenged I learned that although there are not so many Finnish people a majority of them live in Helsinki because of work and community so the city was built at various times to accommodate this.

The city was built by Swedish design and Russian at various times in history so there were lots of big square blocks contrasted by more delicate ornate buildings

The bnb was expensive 39 euros!

I was shocked and called Meg instantly whilst standing at the check in desk then handed the mobile to her so she could talk to the receptionist but there was no shifting from the fee so I put up with it for one night.

I asked Meg to search another for me which she did and then I found myself outside of the main city in a small village place surrounded by countryside. My hostess Outi was very friendly and helpful and showed me places of interest to go like the local beach but it took me ages to understand that these places with long waterways and islands that blocked the long view were not rivers but actually inlets from the sea.

The Helsinki coastline was undermining all my expectations of what a beach should look like and I actually argued with a man when in answer to my question "Where is the beach" said "This is the beach that you re standing on". "No" I insisted "This is not a beach"

I would later discover that Helsinki has many small islands around the coastline.

I did find though the most amazing granite blocks of stone that glittered like jewels and I spent ages looking and being totally fascinated by them some had seams of quartz and others were bejewelled with things I knew of from gem books and I collected the little stones to take back to my grandsons.

These granite rocks I discovered are the foundation of many parts of Finland and I found it perplexing that they are used as ordinary stones with which to build roads because to me they were jewels. There were escalators in the city which proved to be a big challenge for they were twice as long as in London

and the stairs of it are twice as narrow and after enduring my first time on it I did seek out folk to accompany me and I was not fussy about who I asked as this monster was triggering my phobia of heights!

And among the surprised heroes I asked were policemen and well just any one really.

After some journeys on it I would look for a dense group of passengers and wedge myself as tightly as I could in between them (oh yes I got strange looks)

I also discovered that the hand rail to it moved at a faster pace which further made for a feeling of insecurity cos I knew that if one did not move the hand constantly then one was certain that one would end up falling flat on ones face!

Descending was out of the question!

I did find the dock area one day and immediately loved it as the buildings had more character and so were more interesting to me and it was next to the sea and in summer I crave to be near the sea.

There was an open market there for fruit and veg and tourist stuff which was obviously different to UK tourist stuff next to a long row of pop up cafés that sold hot fish food mostly with coffee.

I stopped by a stall selling dried meat and enquired about the identity of the animal "Reindeer" was the reply to which my mind automatically flipped to this thought "Oh No! Not Rudolf the Red Nosed Reindeer!"

I kept my dismay to myself but later when I was a short distance away l heard a very loud English mans voice proclaim "Oh No! Not Rudolf the Red Nosed Reindeer!" and I knew where he was and what he just heard!

Anyone who's English is hot wired to the song of Rudolf the Red Nosed Reindeer as it opens the magic doors to the wonderland of Santa Clause and Christmas and it's a hell of a culture shock to discover otherwise! so I made a note that this was some info to not share with the grandchildren.

There were ferries at this harbour and I took one to an island called Soumenlinna just ten minutes away and we passed by about eight tiny Islands with either small houses or just trees and then tiny smooth granite ones for the birds.

Soumenlinna comprises of five small Islands which are connected by a wooden bridge but one of them is a land bridge .

Soumenlinna

There were tiny Islands dotted about beyond the coastline out to sea but they did not in any way obscure the long view out to the horizon and so at last I was able to enjoy the Full Monty of the beach experience and I loved it.

This place now had become a refuge away from the Helsinki city and it was an extra delight to be able to see the water front of it clearly from the dock area.

Then at night the whole waterfront of Helsinki was all lit up like the jewelled Crown of a Hindu Goddess.

I learned that it was an ancient granite stone fort and now a derelict tourist attraction but there was lots of grass and wild flowers growing all over the Island from the landing dock to the grassy slopes growing over the smooth granite stones down to the sea.

There were many huge granite stone buildings on the Island where it looked like people lived in them.

I was not so focused on the landscape and architecture on this trip as time was short but this island was a refuge to me now away from the big city and I did love the small beaches indeed I did venture to swim in the ocean from a tiny sandy beach and although the sea there was far colder than the UK.

I embraced the experience whole heartedly but I did not venture to put my head under water as that was just a bit too cold for me.

I did note however that the granite stone dominated this island coastline and was different from the glittering beach I had seen as these rocks were smoothed from water and weather which created a whole other art form in its own right and l later wrote a description of this beach.

This tiny sandy beach is a half moon shape which is snuggled at the foot of a grassy hill that wraps itself around it and on either side lay ancient granite stones that sweep down to the sea.

All are very big and smoothed from exposure to eons of weather in Scandinavia and where some of these stones have fallen in to the sea they are now small and rounded by it and seaweed clings to them just above and below the waterline.

This is a peaceful ocean without a tidal system so the seaweed is never too disturbed and wild ducks swim amongst it to feed on the green food.

Another bit of magic was finding large champagne bottle corks on the shore which I collected as they perfectly fitted some glass water bottles I had at home.

Magic Troll Forest

Outi and her husband one fine day took me along with their children to a protected forest in a national park out of town to gather mushrooms we passed many pine trees on the way there and then we slipped into this forest where we found lovely big mushrooms.

Then we came upon a forest area that blew me away completely! for the landscape was straight out of a Faery Tale. The kind that has Trolls!

I was used to English nature where it is soft and green with large deciduous trees that set the scene for some dreamy Arthurian legend where Merlin may just appear and bluebells carpet the woodland in spring beside babbling streams that create a perfect landscape for our mythical Elves and Faery folk to be found.

But here was a huge surprise as I became aware of the very landscape which was the same as the drawings in an old Scandinavian Faery Tale picture book I had

There were pine trees for sure but this landscape was dominated by granite stones some were huge and resembled an elephant or some great strange shape that l fancied could have been a sleeping Troll.

Then there were many small rounded stones that were covered with soft green moss and just showed as little Faery Hills in a very soft green carpet that looked inviting enough to sleep and dream on and these were mixed in with the occasional larger round moss covered stones and in my mind there was this burning question, "How did they become so round"!

It was as if they all had a magic life that they woke up to when the humans weren't looking perhaps they all decided to roll there and maybe they had spent eons just rolling around Scandinavia till they found their perfect home.

And in that mystical landscape l was ready to believe a magic tale such as that one.

One thing was clear to me l was not sure how comfortable l would feel to be there alone in the dark but in daylight I was enchanted by this new form of nature and felt privileged to experience it.

Outi's family gathered some great mushrooms and I was impressed to hear that most Finnish children can identify the edible ones.

I did take as many photos as possible before leaving and made a plan to return asap.

Tova Janssen

Back in the city l had discovered the art museum (Ateneum) which was this year putting on an exhibition of Tova Janssens art work to celebrate her hundredth birthday as she is an Icon and the creator of the Moomins.

I happened to mention this to Megi on the mobile who was most delighted "She's my hero" she said and I was amazed at the coincidence and delighted as it gave me an opportunity to buy her lots of Tova art stuff as a thank you for all her help.

I also searched out the metal merchandise shop in Kaampi which seemed a version of Londons Soho and I could not find a good Wintersun t shirt but at least I tried.

Roveniemi

Then I wanted to travel a bit and Outi remembered an Airbnb friend in Roveniemi which is a big town up in the north so I booked an all night train and arrived next morning.

The roomy building I stayed in was where the family sauna cabin was also and I learned how the sauna played such an important role in the family that when building a house they would build the wood smoke sauna room first sometimes outside and sometimes in the centre and then build the house around it as it was the bathroom and the birthing room and it kept the home warm in 30 degree below temperature.

In the Roveniemi library they were celebrating the life of Tova Jannsen with a film that I watched and despite it being in Finnish I did enjoy it as she was an accomplished artist with a brave spirit.

This city was very, very small compared to Helsinki with quiet a lot built on a long hill where I found a large river at the bottom of it under a very big state of the art bridge and I made it my swimming place.

I took a walk along the river bank which was lined with birch trees one day.

My dream of engaging in conversation about Finnish Faery tales came to nought as I discovered that most Fins did not like to talk so I tried to connect with this new nature, albeit a strange one to me and when I found a long row of birch trees beside the river, I respectfully put my hands on one and rested my head against it to connect with its Spirit.

This was far more than I had hoped for as l did experience a colour for the Spirit of the tree that was a beautiful magenta and when l walked back along the line l caught site of an unusual oak tree that looked a bit like an old Faery Tale Witch as its branches were skinny and gnarled like aged arms and fingers one of which was seeming to point in a direction close by.

My friend Outi had given me a piece of a fungus harvested from a birch tree because it made a medicinal tea which she called Puukeri! and asked me to look for it and I made many attempts to say the word properly till I got it sorted.

I followed the line of the pointed finger branch and found it was directed at a fungus growing on a birch tree close by and it was a fungus that looked just like the piece I had and l was delighted and marked this as the first treasure as I cut it out with my penknife. Magic! I had not thought too much about the birch tree before but I was now beginning to respect it, indeed much later I learned that the Indigenous Race of the Sami relied on it to survive.

There is a square in Roveniemi that was renamed Lordi Square after the Young Metal Music Band who won the Eurovision song contest as they all were natives to the city and I saw their hand prints in bedded in the stone and concrete pillar which amused me.

Arctic Circle

I was discovering also that I was just a few kilometres from the Arctic Circle where THE Santa Clause was so I caught the local bus, paid just 7 euros and in a short time I was there. Wow!

Another culture shock because in my imagination this was a forest landscape with a small wooden Santa Clause hut!

Yes Santa's office has big wooden doors and there's a wooden sign post showing how far away London and other places were but progress had arrived and there were many shops and cafés set around a large circle with Arctic Circle painted on the ground and three lots of numbers depicting degrees North I presumed.

Yoonas the Sami Boy

Then just outside the circle in a pine forested area I saw my very first Sami in the shape of a young man who was looking after the Reindeer he was a handsome boy and wearing the traditional Sami clothes of a woven blue wool hat and a blue and gold tunic which he told me was an antique.

I was enthusiastic about communicating with him and he was friendly, he said his family had the rights to building a big sauna and café in the wooded area l saw also a travelling Sami dwelling which resembled a Tipi there.

As I wanted to connect and talk with him I played the tourist game and paid 5 euros to follow him and feed a reindeer that was rather young and small and was really not interested in taking the branch from my outstretched hand so I just took some pics of us all.

I did discover from Yoonas that being able to trace your Sami Grandmother was now advantageous as land rights may be respected and he showed me a partly-built wooden structure that would become a café and sauna when completed.

I invited Yoonas to friend me on Fb before leaving.

Crystal Man

Then I walked into the nearby forest just around the Sami space and saw edible mushrooms growing amidst green carpeted forest floor alive with blueberries and of course the little and bigger round stones.

I bought family gifts and wondered into the Top shop which was next to Santa Clause's residence and it was very light with lots of large and best I'd ever seen good quality amethyst geodes.

I attracted some attention from a young man as I was taking pictures of them then his father appeared and this was Wolfgang, who is German, and a larger than life friendly characterwith a big beard and smile to match who manages the shop and café there so I engaged him in friendly conversation and then I noticed that he had a deep connection with the crystals and stones so I recognised him as a crystal man and made that known to him.

We connected on a deeper level now and I was handling some black polished stones called shungite which I had not seen before. Wolfgang disappeared for a short time and when he returned he gifted me with some shungite powder and rough stone also.

He did say something about it but I was not listening properly and it was months before I looked on line and discovered what a treasure it was and so that was my second treasure.

I had lunch there and he spoke to me about the Northern Lights and he loved them very much he then after some time of talking leaned over a little to me as he held my gaze and said in a more intense but focused way "Go North because everything below the Arctic Circle is Just Africa"!

Well I d not heard that before! and it was delivered with such authority that I really felt compelled to actually go North.

I had no plans made and it was September the 9th but I was not due to return home till the 17th so I booked a coach to the northern most point called Inari.

A friendly girl in the tourist centre told me that soon the sky would be clear enough to see the Northern lights which surprised me as I thought it had to be mid winter for that to occur.

METAL MYSTICS TAKE ME

At the coach station I met a few young students who were on their way to Norway to learn about the Sami peoples and we became friends but when we arrived in Inari approx six hours later.

Kiara Frida and Selma stayed on the coach.

Inari

I was alone and as I had not booked any place to stay I was feeling vulnerable and again this place looked bleak at first sight as I struggled to understand how one tiny hotel and a few buildings were A Town!

I was feeling defeated and vulnerable so I called Megan to say I wanted to go home then two really friendly Lithuanian woman who were on holiday with their dogs rescued me and took me to a camp site up the road a bit where I made myself comfortable in a small wooden chalet being careful now to call Megan again in a more positive mode.

There were other chalets and showers and a sauna hut also and all this was set close to a very big ancient lake with moored boats.

There were good showers and of course a smoke sauna hut by the lake which I did not use that time but I did see folk going to the lake after a sauna and diving in.

I sat and watched the sunset on a wooden landing pad at the edge of the lake and it was so alive with colours of gold and purple that I believed I may be seeing the actual Northern Lights.

The sunset was very slow to dim out and I stayed till the very end when the sky turned to a romantic light purple.

I was not usually fond of still lakes as I prefer moving water such as oceans and rivers but I made a big exception for this lake as it was huge with small hills lining one side that entirely enhanced the sun sets and set the water of the wind swept lake ablaze with a rippling symphony of golds, blues, purples and reds.

Then later in the gathering darkness the breeze gently blowing on the lake set it shimmering like a silver jewel where the full moon poured down its reflection of light into the small billows of the water.

I could have stayed all night to watch but sleep called me and I had to obey.

The next morning was sunny and warm as I walked to the town I passed many pine trees and wild flowers on the side of a nearly deserted road.

Sami Museum

Across the bridge in the town I found the Sami museum which I was thrilled to discover.

I spent sometime there learning about the Indigenous Sami people who travelled with the Reindeer and were masters of surviving long dark winters and I saw more about the birch tree.

The museum was built tall with wood with large glass windows that ensured good and lighting the front part held a large shop where Sami clothes books cards and prints were sold.

I bought some big black and white prints of Sami life like a baby swaddled in a basket that was strapped over a reindeer's back which I gave to Morgana later and a couple sitting on the earth outside their temporary home which was built quiet like a Tipi in shape and this I gave to my daughter Indra.

Outside around the back of the museum they had built the more modern version of the Sami dwelling that was a strong and small wooden house with a striking chimney set in a corner expertly rounded and made of stones.

Looking into these dwellings showed the fire place had a raised hearth for cooking on I read about their culture and I became more familiar with their spiritual beliefs and my fascination and respect just kept growing.

They were masters of surviving the extreme temperatures and cold dark winters but not in sadness or fear rather with a joy of connection to nature that mostly only Indigenous Tribes enjoy.

They had their own music which was something like a spontaneous chanting to honour nature and I became most upset to learn about how their Pagan connection with nature made them a target for persecution from the new Christian settlers.

I spent time at the camp site and saw for the first time blueberries growing freely amidst a startling array of lichen with all colours of green in a masterpiece of natural art from Mother Nature and this magic carpet was all around and probably all over Finland as about ninety percent is given to natural forest.

Northern Lights

Around 8 pm in the evening I was standing outside looking at a beautiful bright full moon and a voice behind me spoke saying "You're in luck be here at midnight." That was the manager and I knew he was talking about the Northern Lights so I took a place outside quiet early and observed the sky and he very kindly made sure that I was out on time.

There was a brilliant full moon shining like a huge pearl against a bright blue sky which was clear except for one thin white long cloud with a hook on the end of it that I found really strange because I had not ever seen that before and it remained quiet still high above my head for the whole four hours I was outside.

Then at the stroke of midnight I looked up to see the thin white cloud with the hook like hand suddenly began to move and glide like a serpent.

And then right in front of my amazed eyes it danced in huge flowing waves and spirals across the beautiful clear dark blue sky and all in an incandescent and brilliant bright white light.

And I was transfixed with head thrown back watching in complete awe.

I have heard it said that the Northern lights make their own music and in my place of imaginings I fancied that I could hear it.

There were not the usual long veils as I think it was too early in the year but it revealed more of the architectural aspects which showed up every minute detail of the white incandescent shining spiraled movements as clear as you could see under a microscope and perfectly framed against the dark blue of the sky.

And it covered the whole sky as it danced in this way for one full hour in exquisite gliding Serpent like moves across a perfect blue sky witnessed by the jewelled pearl of a special full moon.

This Force of Nature was so powerful that it almost overwhelmed me and certainly there was no place for my logical mind to interfere with the magical majesty of it.

All my inspiration and visions came from my imagination and here I was witnessing the very stuff that visions are made of and I had no reference for it in my mind and certainly this divine vision was far too big to comprehend with a logical structure.

So all I could do was stand and stare and willingly surrender everything I ever thought was me to just be empty of mind to enable this phenomenal Force of Nature to reach every part of my being.

And that is just what I did.

When ever the white serpent dance seemed to fade there then poured down great fine and delicate white shards of beaming light between the white serpent trails and this phenomenon created another dynamic dance and was as startling in its majesty and beauty as the Serpent Dance.

And deep inside me a realization stirred that this felt like the closest I have been to seeing with my human eyes a real live Divine Goddess that existed out side of my imagination and it caused me to wonder if this was the White Goddess that I saw in my Visions before I started this journey.

And that was followed by another realization that I was probably witnessing the very Origins of Sacred Dance itself.

And I was certain that this all beautiful mystical and powerful Natural Force was Eternal and was for ever out of the reach of any human will and would never be controlled by any human intervention.

And with that knowing also I realised fully what the impact of feeling Awestruck really felt like. Absolutely No Words.

And for one hour my head was fixed in an upturned position just following with my eyes. And I knew that this experience changed me for ever now.

When it was finally over I reclaimed my head and fell into bed exhausted and slept.

Sacred Lake

The Inari Lake is Sacred to the Sami and I had promised that I d swim naked in the lake if I saw the Lights and the next morning that's what I did after finding a secret place and the water was not too cold and the act of this swimming marked a completion of a strange and mystical journey.

Talk of Metal with Selma

It was also leaving day and as I waited for the coach by the road side I saw that the whole forest was full of blueberries amongst the amazing carpets of green lichen so I gathered some and passed them around on the bus.

I was pleasantly surprised to see my young friends again on the bus and Frida said she d seen the Northern Lights in green in Norway and cried!

She had said earlier that she was born in Helsinki grew up there but never saw the lights, "How sad" I thought "To miss the most magical natural show on earth when it was all around to see" but so glad that Frida saw it all.

I counted the Northern Lights experience as my third treasure.

I talked with Selma a lot on that journey and she loved metal music and she said that one metal music fan will easily recognise another so I found that interesting as it added a depth to the energy of metal music fans which was of interest to me as this was my first real discussion about metal music cos in the UK I would mostly listen on my own to my metal band on the bus with earplugs.

We all separated in Helsinki and I realised I d left my coats on the bus so Angel Outi made phone calls and I retrieved them at Kaampi coach station then when I was putting them on I forgot my camera was on the ground and walked away from it.

But an old Rumanian beggar woman called to me to say what I had done and saved it from disappearing from my life so I collected my camera with all pics and videos of my adventure and was so grateful that I gave five Euros to her. I was aware that she could have walked away with it and I was touched by this event and she spoke Italian to me which is my mother's language and that resonated emotionally. Another beggar girl who'd seen this event ran over to me with her grandmother asking for money and I was in such a good mood now that i took her to the local supermarket and offered her 5 euros for food.. Sorted.

Birthday on Haraka

It was then my birthday and I was taking a boat to a small island just five minutes away and I don't remember why but I met with a stone artist who had a workshop in the big building there and she made me birthday tea and told me of the history of the island.

The Germans used it as an experimental laboratory during the war and years later it was transformed into a nature reserve and artist community and I spent hours following her around looking at small stones.

Eons ago there were fires made on the granite stones next to the sea leaving evidence of burnt places which I liked a lot as my interest is always prehistory time.

Metal Pub

At some time whilst in Helsinki I wondered up aside road of the main city road and came across a Metal Music pub it had a big front window and a name on the door in Finnish that I couldn't make out but the inside had a comfortable sofa and a big bar with a friendly barman and just a few young metal folk sitting at tables. There was a cellar below where they would host new up and coming metal bands and the doors opened at 10 30pm entrance fee was just 3 Euros to hang your coat so I ventured down.

Tables, high stools, a stage at the back and a long colourful bar with pictures of metal celebrity's on the walls related a warmth there.

I waited till the young metal musician took centre stage to play full on heavy metal music on electric guitar and I stayed as long as I could to honour his efforts till my ears screamed for mercy!

In a confined place loud metal music can be deafening but I was glad for the experience and I noted the metal pub as an oasis of friendly folk.

One great thing about Helsinki is that buses run till 2 30 in the morning and my last bus home was just a bit before and there would be future times where I'd be grateful for that.

I connected one last time with Kiara and Frida and took them to Soumenlinna island where we sat on a large quartz stone and watched the sun set for the last time and I realised that I was sad to leave this island now after three weeks in Finland this was my favourite place.

METAL MYSTICS TAKE ME

I was aware of the absence of connecting live with Wintersun in Helsinki but I felt so new to this adventure that was in its early days so patience was asked of me.

AAAAHHH!

I arrived back home and rested for a day or two before looking at two streaks of white light on my iPhone.

Then I looked the pictures and videos in my camera.

When I did I was dismayed to discover that the camera wouldn't translate the Northern Lights scene and then my memory of it unbelievably was a blank as if my logical mind was refusing to show me what I d seen (which on reflection was understandable as another part of me was experiencing the event.)

I was caught out now as I always relied on my camera to record nature scenes for me and it was effectively my memory and now I could not recall just what I had seen I could not deal with the problem just then as the disappointment cut really deep.

Goddess Sketch

I could not bear the thought of losing that very special experience so I just left the problem hanging whilst I went foraging for wild berries for a few weeks which is something I do each Autumn. I gave my family all the gifts I had bought them.

This year I made the usual Hawthorn berry leathers that were an ancient stone age food and a heart tonic along with Elder Berry potion for the winter and later Chestnut and Walnut gathering.

Then on January 1st I sat at a table with pencil and paper and decided to at least attempt to draw the energy of what I had seen as I needed to at least honour the experience.

I remembered the emotional aspect well enough and that the Lights had a Goddess like impression of immense power and passion and the movement of it reminded me of Sacred Dance so I just put all these attributes together in my mind and let my pencil be guided by my intuition.

The result of which I am so very grateful for still today!

What emerged from my pencil was a simple drawing of approx twelve aspects of a Goddess in a serpent like dance.

These Images did appear to show me the dynamic and Divine passionate energy of the event and I was so delighted with the effect that I was inspired to write a poem, which I did and it just flowed off the pen just like it had been waiting to be written (as if by some Magic) then I put the two together in a printed card with a plan to take them to Finland to give away. (Later the memory of the lights did return)

METAL MYSTICS TAKE ME

The Northern Lights

A Vision of the White Goddess took me
To the Land of the Midnight Sun
In Lapland where I stood by Inari Ancient Lake
That I may catch a glimpse of the Blessed One

In that Moon Kissed Midnight Place
With Longing Heart and Upturned Face
I surrendered all I Knew
My Thoughts like Ancient Warriors
All Falling at the Alter of Her Beauty To receive Her State of Grace

Then above my Head in the Temple of Night
A Thin White Cloud with Hook like Hand did Ley
And Suddenly did Move and Dance Exquisitely
And Serpent like in Waves and Spirals Across a Perfect Indigo Sky

Being Early of Year the Billowing White Veils
Were not yet Long Revealing more of a Cosmic Architectural Stance
And as they Glided Majestically Through the Velvet Night
I did Believe that I was Witness to The Origins of Sacred Dance

Then Beams of Light like Cast off Veils
Came Pouring Down from Unseen Hands
And Joined the Holy Dance in the Wake of Winged Trails
Mysteriously they did Glide and Fall The Cosmic Beams amid Flowing Strands
Till my Eyes were Filled with Visions of the White Goddess
In this Most Mystical of Lands

Now to tell the Tale I Wave my Hand in Serpent-like Mimicry
As Ancient Dancers may have Done
To Show what Mind Cannot Translate
In Presence of Divinity

Plan B Holiday

(Later the logical memory of the Northern Lights experience did return to me)

I felt I now had some idea to show people who lived in Helsinki how great the Northern Lights were in the hopes of inspiring them to travel to see them.

Now my spiritual journey was being guided by the fruits of my artistic expression and that felt good.

I remembered to surf the net for Puukeri and discovered it is also known as Chaga and just when Id gotten the hang of saying Puukeri and it was the Only Finnish word I could pronounce.

Then I surfed the net for shungite and when I found it. What a treasure that was and it changed my plans cos now I wanted to go to Russian Karelia which is where it's from and swim in the shungite lakes and visit the shungite caves Ambitious plan? Oh Yes. So I planned to arrive in Helsinki the next summer stay for a few days before getting a coach to Russian Karelia where I would camp near all the great shungite lakes and swim in them, so I obviously forgot what a pain camping was and bought a tent etc and a festival trolley to transport it all on which I did think was pretty organised of me. (It was a real pukka festival trolley incidentally)

I took another plane to Helsinki on the 30th of July and again some ones clumsiness got my camera broke but I had a 15 mega pixel camera on a new mobile phone which would be my camera now.

It was the 1st of August but! I had no idea that I needed a visa and so it all went wrong and I was in Helsinki being refused.

Meg had advised me to take a diary this time and with it the first entries chronologically tracked the hopeless visits to various authorities where my request was refused.

I did find a Fat Hen plant though growing beautifully near a wall close to the

Russian embassy, it's a Stone Age plant and has more nutritional value than spinach and cabbage and in the UK I will travel some distance to find it and I was reminded of the value of the simple things in life.

I think I surrendered to my fate and began to search for a plan B holiday and I'd contacted Outi already to stay for a short while which I did do and in that brief time span.

Ergo at Metal Pub

I once again visited the metal music pub with a strong resolve to engage someone in a conversation about Scandinavian Faery Tales.

I sat on the comfy sofa and introduced myself to Ergo who was a good looking young man and I bought an organic beer after asking the barman if I could take a photo of him, a request he graciously agreed to and he made a metal symbol with his hand as he held the beer bottle which I thought had real style.

The beer was so strong I gave most of it away to Ergo.

My diary says that we talked about deep soul stuff and coincidently he was from Finnish Karelia but the thing I remember most was him telling me that his favourite thing was to crash out after drinking a lot of beer.

Magic Ateneum

The Ateneum was host to Magic Art this year and I thought that was great as the first year was for Meg and this was my year.

The Ateneum I believe was once a very posh aristocrats mansion and the interior certainly bears this out as it has the classic features like a long marble staircase which I could not climb as it triggered my phobia of heights.

There's a huge hanging poster on the outside of the Ateneum which showcases one the paintings being shown and this year it was a painting of Jack Frost that was so imaginatively and sensitively painted that it was a wonder for my eyes and this magic Elemental was also one of the main characters in the magic book I wrote for my grandchildren that I'd given to Teemu Mäntysaari.

In my book the children were dressed each according to the role played and we had a Faery Queen a Dragon Queen, Jack Frost an Elf a Dragon Prince and a Pink Faery.

There was a painting in the Ateneum that was inspired by a book called the Kalevala which is considered to be a National treasure Indeed the Finnish composer Sibelius wrote music that was inspired by it.

The painting was of three maidens with sort of punkish sticking up in the air orange hair and I put it as a painting I wish I had created.

I also fell in love with a painting of a really beautiful bleak snow scene that just drew me right in to it untill I felt I was the strange bird in the picture perched on a high branch in the snow covered pine tree as snow flakes fell quietly around me.

Lime Blossom of Soumenlinna

I also wrote. "Soumenlinna at last again" As I set first foot on the island it was the beginning of August and I'd heard that the summer was only just now beginning so the blue sky was a therapy and the real clouds were a joy to see.

The ferry to Soumenlinna begins at the Helsinki dock area where it is possible to use your bus pass for the ride.

It is a slow and almost silent trip where at the back and front of the boat are outside areas where it is possible to lean over the end a little to see all the foam that's created by the boat moving through the flat and constant calm water.

The seascape is an adventure in its self as directly on the left is the huge Viking line ferry which is either arriving from Sweden or just leaving and people on the top deck usually wave and I did enjoy waving back.

To the right of the harbour are some small wooden piers to receive more much smaller local sea ferries visiting the many small islands that are dotted about the sea.

Then further away to the right is the other ferry that goes to Estonia and then we are sailing as we take the left side out passing these remarkable tiny islands that on the right side form a chain with only a short distance of water in between and much later I would be considering swimming from one to another but only on a very special occasion like a birthday.

Some of these islands have trees and small wooden cabins where people actually live and then there's the really tiny island of smooth granite stone that is the large nesting birds domain.

Nearing Soumenlinna one can see evidence of the five islands that make up the one as on the far right the connecting wooden bridge is visible and on that far tiny island is the home of the Finnish Navy, complete with waving flag set on the roof of a very big square stone granite building.

There is another smaller island next to that one that is invisible from the dock but there is a smaller wooden bridge connection and in that area are really big stone buildings in a block given over for flats.

Then walking through them is the far right beach with big smoothed granite stone dipping down into the ocean.

Back at the landing dock of Soumenlinna there is a wide path leading in all directions which is also home to a very long granite building that has a big clock tower and a huge arch way leading to the main middle island complex of granite buildings.

This place is now restaurants art galleries a small museum of information with a tourist room and is painted pink then walking through the archway on ancient cobbled stones that lead up a little and left revealing some old wooden houses at the side of this path.

On the left out side the ice cream hut is the most adorable ancient water pump that needs some skill to make work and if you are willing to risk getting soaked with the out pouring water your efforts will be rewarded with the sweetest tasting water. Once I had discovered this hidden treasure I would fill my water bottle from it when ever I was there, which was most days.

On this small island are tiny cafés living apartments grass and the biggest lime trees I have ever seen and there are little museum rooms set in the granite fort and from this place one could walk down to the sailing boat harbour where a very long line of sailing boats come and go a lot in summer all belong to residents I think and the main visitor centre is there also.

Walking over the next wooden bridge which connects a sea inlet flanked either side by the old fort there is a view of a small island which at certain times is totally dwarfed by the Viking ferries sailing behind it.

From this island over the bridge are many remnants visible of the might of the fortress and its clear to see that the walls were unbelievably thick leading to a labyrinth of damp and sometimes dripping granite corridors.

Further on there are more places in the walls that reveal big spaces where now they have been fashioned for theatrical shows and I did see glass making in one of these secret spaces and some are become tiny museums now.

I just had to visit the really small submarine nestled at the edge of the ocean where 3 euros would allow a wander through and I took lots of pics for my grandsons and it really was an inspiration for how to live comfortably in a small space.

Great big smooth granite stones surround Soumenlinna either up high on the paths and dipping down to the sea in layers which make perfect ledges for sitting on with a picnic with the family whilst enjoying a beautiful sea view and this is where most families would sit as there was not much beach area on the shore.

I found my way to the one and only small sandy beach and this year it was a delight to see there were wild ducks with chicks and lots of children enjoying the sea and sand.

I noticed the nature more this year and as it was earlier in August now I was able to see the many huge lime trees with blossoms that infused the air with their scent and to me this was an exquisite experience.

Soumenlinna Hostel

There were many wild geese on the island and they feasted on the small green Plantain that also grows where I live but in my land I am the gatherer of this humble looking weed and I make raw chips from them as they are full of goodness and incidentally the leaves when crushed and rubbed on to the skin will ease nettle sting and cure all manner of skin problems, but here on this island I left it to the geese.

I was pleased to see Meadowsweet Jack by the Hedge which is edible Yarrow for fever and Tansy which was used in England for flavouring puddings and has some value medicinally when used carefully.

Outi had been away but when she returned there was a full house and I had to leave which I accepted as I should not be there but camping in Russian Karelia now.

Of course I felt insecure about where to stay now so I decided to spend a few nights at the hostel on Soumenlinna while I thought on the next move and I was able to book two nights.

My hostel room had about ten bunk beds was as big as most other rooms were as this social use of buildings is a departure from the original intentions of an antique army fort 25 euros did feel excessive to pay but my need outweighed the politics of the situation and I acknowledged it to be a unique experience as well.

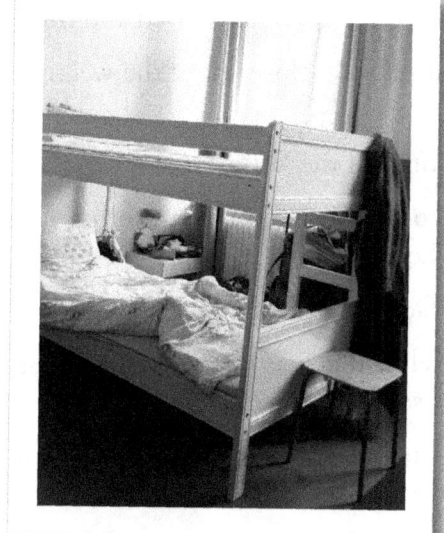

Speaking of Eluveiti

The first night the room was empty except for myself and a Swiss girl who was so tall that she could not fit on the bed properly and another coincidence was that not only was she a metal music fan but she had known Crigle who was the lead singer in the folk metal band Eluveiti! Before he became an international folk metal star and this was the very first band that was recommended to me at Summerbreeze where I first saw crowd surfing at his gig wow what a coincidence. I did understand from that festival that the more popular the music band then the more crowd surfing occurred and there was multiple crowd surfing at Eluveitis gig Indeed there were two devoted fans waving a Swiss flag whilst crowd surfing and I remember feeling admiration for their great sense of style.

Eluvieti is the ancient name for Switzerland and Crigle is the song writer he learned his own ancient Pagan Gaulish language to sing his songs in and he is a musician who can confidently play any instrument and he sings of the ancient Pagan way of life death celebration and rebirth all influenced by the Ancient Gods and Goddesses of Gaul.

He exchanged the way of being a classical Folk musician for Folk Metal and he brought all his skills with him for playing Mandolin and Flute.

His other band members play the hurdy gurdy electric guitar violin bagpipes and drums.

The Silver Sister is a song I later got and loved and here are some words from it:

> The Silvern Light a stannite glow under the welkin dark solemn chants will soar.

> The Immemorial songs of the Wise.

> To declare the rise of the night-born of glinting dew and Surunnant winds of a vibrant dawn Long for shown.

> And your Pristine face pours down Crystal Rays

> Caressed by your Velvet touch as we dance through the night One last Silver Kiss as the Ancient song falls silent.

> Your Radiance Crystalline Heralds the ancient Words Resounding high and Clear from the Other World.

> In this Night we Dance Glory to the Nameless One.

These are just some of the lyrics and the whole song can be heard on YouTube.

All the Eluvietie words and music can be found on YouTube.

Still no connecting with Wintersun but Eluveiti helped to keep the Metal Music energy alive.

Syncronistic Ware Wolf

I found myself playing a strange game called Werewolf with some very pleasant European students on my last night at the hostel, its too complicated to explain here but its a kind of big whodunit guessing game and synchronistically my granddaughter Morgana related to me that she had played that game for the first time on that very same night as myself in the UK.

Ghosts of Soumenlinna

On arrival in Helsinki I had lost no time in giving away my Northen Lights cards which I was gratified to see were received very well and on Soumenlinna this giving of cards continued with me standing on the main path just handing them around.

Around the time of my hostel adventure two navel officers were walking past and I offered them a card each.

They introduced themselves as Staff Lieutenant Juhana and Captain Elleryelf! Of course the Captains name was not quiet that but his actual name eluded me as some Finnish names do cos it's the speed at which they are said that loses me so l wrote what if sounded like.

We talked about the Northern lights and the Captain told me that his favourite colour was red as it lit up the sky like a big ruby. Meanwhile Lt Juhana was looking at the poem.

I need to say here about how incredibly handsome they both were the Captain was tall and blonde and Lt Juhana was also tall with brown haunting eyes and a green heart energy and wow that got my attention in a big way.

I borrowed the Captain's pencil to write my email on the cards but forgot to return it and then they left.

It was around this time I learned that Soumenlinna island became a prison of war camp in the 1917 civil war and of the 5000 men who were detained there only 1000 survived due to the dreadful conditions to go back home alive.

It was also about this time that I experienced some thing of a ghostly apparition that quiet stunned me because suddenly in broad daylight I saw some spirits of the men who clearly did not leave!

They were weaving through the big granite stone wall of the fort then something really unexpected happened (I felt a pain in my heart for them).

I was so emotionally effected by this Other Worldly Event that I missed writing it in my diary as I was really puzzled as to why I had been chosen to witness the apparition and to actually feel it so deeply but I felt compelled to do something to help these suffering souls to go home.

I knew nothing about if there had been a commemorative service for them and I didn't feel confidant in talking of it being Pagan so I decided to honour them in my own way and write a magic story where they do go home.

Story Telling Stones of Soumenlinna

It seemed fitting that I ask the Spirits of the island for inspiration if I was back home in UK I would walk to the forest I knew and stand by the stream but here on this island I grew to understand that the Stones Ruled.

So I made a mermaid on the sandy beach and then walked to the other side where there were big smooth flat granite stones just resting in and out of the sea and I chose one and lay down on it pressing the side of my face onto it and then resting the palms of my hands on it and waited a short while until my patience and belief was rewarded and a story began weaving its way from out of the stone and into being!

I had the Captain's pencil which became my magic story writing yellow pencil then I rushed to the small post office to beg some scrap of paper in order to begin the story.

A very kind girl there gladly gave me about 20 large pieces of blank paper and I felt the story get stronger as I rushed to the small sandy beach to begin writing.

The haunting eyes of Lt Juhana transformed him into my muse for the story and in no time at all I had written the basic outline of the story.

A chance meeting with Kiara's mother in the metro affirmed my desire to go to some Karelia even the Finnish one as she mentioned it and it is a testament to the small amount of people of this land that she recognised my red hair description from Kiara and also to how few women have red hair also.

New Friends

Outi booked a coach and I was ready to go but just before departing I met Unis who is an artist and Saun her husband and their son Chris they remembered me from the previous year swimming in the sea and for a while we were friends.

I was invited to their home which was one of the artist flats and I was impressed with the work that Shaun had done to turn it from a big empty shell of a room to a big living comfortable home with an open fire place.

There were two big windows and as the room was on a corner they had two separate views of the sea scape.

They had a ginger cat that they walked to the beach daily on a long string and a sailing boat that the family would all sail around and the islands in.

I was there one day when Saun was racing against many other competitors it was a special day with a festival atmosphere and I enjoyed it.

Karelia

Then I travelled to Karelia I had some name of a place to Matila in Koli but the coach stopped in Joensu at midnight and I walked for one hour to a strange camp site in the city well it was amongst some trees and in a green area and I was really tired.

I tried for more than one hour to put up the tent then gave up and asked the aid of a man who appeared on a bike but unfortunately he was drunk and more trouble than I needed so I just threw the damn tent together in some kind of state and fell into it promising to never bring a tent again.

The next morning I walked to the train station where there was a café and to my relief it was run by two alternative folk who helped me arrange a taxi to my destination later. I relaxed for a while and went to an open market where I bought a small Iron pan for cooking mushrooms and I saw a real pair of Sami boots.

I was determined to hunt for mushrooms and blueberries and I was tempted to buy the boots but I was trying to economise so I didn't.

I had seen a video at the Ateneum showing how the Sami would gather a long special grass and comb it all out and then fashion it to fit inside the boots which protected the feet from cold and damp.

Then the taxi arrived and I was away the driver did not speak English so I had to ask for help at a hotel where he tried to drop me so then I was outside a small pub managed by a French man who gave me directions to my destination bnb.

I tried to walk up the hill shown with trolley but it was hot and I was fed up so decided to walk back to the road and stick my thumb out because I wanted to leave and I decided to sleep on the road side if necessary and this option seemed likely as there was no traffic on this road but after ten minutes a big rover turned up and a woman rescued me.

Old Smoked Sauna Cabin

Her name was Lisa and she took me back to her home and within the hour I was sitting inside a 100 year old Old Smoke Sauna Cabin with her and being offered beer. "What were the chances of that" I mused gratefully.

I was most relieved to be safe and comfortable and the sauna cabin was very impressively fashioned in wood with one wood burning stove that black stones adorned around the top of it then when water was carefully dribbled on them, they released steam that looked like smoke and aided the sweating process but also created a rare atmosphere which you might see in an old oil painting perhaps.

Lisa said that this was also the bathroom and I saw some small wooden buckets and soaps and clothes and there was a higher wooden shelf but we sat on the wooden floor.

After a time of soaking up the experience, she invited me to pour water on the stones big mistake! cos I poured on too much and we had to leave rather fast as billows of really hot steam hissed forth. (Foreigners do that she sighed kindly)

We then both swam in a large pond next to the cabin and Lisa said that she swims in it every day as well as in winter and it was sublime after the initial cold rush.

Her husband Jukka was tending a small barbecue and kindly offered me the last sausage which I could not refuse even though in life I never eat those things but in Finland they are common food then l listened as their story unfolded.

They are both artist and crafts man and they moved here from Helsinki some years before Lisa designed fabric and Jukka was a master craftsman working with stone, wood and metal, indeed his workshop was an Aladdin's cave of rare treasures like examples of his work and all the specialist tools and neatly placed.

The landscape was different here with more green soft rolling hills and fields with small stacks of tied corn in them and I learnt that the two Karelias used to be one place.

There is an artist trail through the forest to a big lake and both these folk created it and they put this place Koli on the artistic map Koli was the name of the nearby mountain as well as the area. So this is the artistic royalty who rescued me from the road, lucky me! The very late summer start had taken its toll and there was depletion of energy and depression in people there I made a note of that.

Koli Mountain

Lisa took me up the Koli mountain which was named in three parts, the first being Baby Koli the second was Mother Koli and the last was Father Koli and somewhere there was the name Ukker Koli but I was too busy managing a phobia to pay much attention to it.

I'd warned her about my phobia for heights and she was very careful and helpful and we did manage to arrive at the top of Mother Koli without too much trouble.

The story of the mountain began when lots of molten rock flowed until it rose up to form this mountain and it was of a white rare granite stone.

The view which I gazed at from a safe distance away was overlooking a really huge lake dotted with tiny islands many which Lisa had travelled to in winter. This mountain was really big but was dressed all around in grasses and small trees and time and the feet of folk had created a well defined series of paths so walking up was easy.

I noticed later whilst walking around that Lisa's garden was mostly green plants and a small vegetable plot and from this the top of the garden there was a perfect view of the strangest sight I have ever seen in any garden which was quiet mind blowing and positively surreal!

For at the bottom of it there suddenly rose up a very wide and high steep mountain side covered with pine trees that did seem to reach to the very sky!

The house was old, wooden and had bags of character with a huge wood burning stove about six foot wide in the large kitchen which did look like it would certainly keep toes and noses warm in the winter.

I enjoyed Lisa's hospitality for two days and then she drove me up to my earlier intended destination at Matila, where earlier I had abandoned the path to it and it was far better reaching it by car.

This place had a bigger wooden house set in a large garden area that was surrounded by the forest trees, most of which were pine. There was a small barn area converted into individual sleeping rooms which is where I was offered a space and there was of course the sauna hut and compost loo!

Kai and Ilka were the managers and they held the space all summer being host to different workshops and spiritual events and the breakfast made were a work of devotional art using the edible flowers and green things that grew in the garden to adorn it.

I followed the path at the top of the garden that went through the forest, and it was there that I saw the artistic work of Lisa and Jukka in the form of big weatherproof sculptures on the side of the path and I think it was called the Art Trail!

Lisa had told me they'd created an Artist's Residency for artists to stay at the hotel for a time to work.

This walk took about half an hour and it ended with a path leading down to the great lake side where there was a shore and a stone wall for boats to moor by, and it had also changing huts for swimmers.

There was a big sort of wooden hotel with a restaurant which hosted many Russian families.

I did swim a little which was pleasant then whilst sunbathing I was bitten by mosquitoes URGHH! They have no manners cos they'll bite through your clothes and I had to not scratch (all thirty bites I counted).

Much later I did realise that if I had succeeded in going to the lakes to swim in Russian Karelia in August I probably would have been eaten alive by them!

Shakti Dance

Later that day I met Daniel and Natalie at Matila who were from Switzerland and enjoyed walking in remote places decided to spend a couple of nights there.

Natalie taught yoga and Daniel was a kind of builder as his day job but something very special also as he had a rare perceptive ability which I did admire greatly. They brought red wine and offered it around and I gave them the card of my picture and poem to which Natalie remarked after studying it.

"Shakti Dance!" I had heard the name before as it was the name given to sacred dance.

Well l was delighted that she thought that about my drawing and then later when Kai asked if I was thinking of painting it, l was taken along another direction with this art and pondered this idea as a real possibility.

Daniel and Natalie showed me something on line called The Human Design System which was a kind of energy diagnostic system that worked from the physical right up to the metaphysical all that is required is you tap in the time of birth and date and l was really impressed with the result.

Stone Sacrifice

The following day they both took me up the Koli mountain again beginning with Baby Koli and as I'd warned them both about my phobia Daniel said he'd pick a stone to sacrifice up the top for it.

Great stuff really! Any how I planted myself firmly between them and we began our journey to the top of the mountain and upon reaching the top Daniel saw a tiny cave just off the edge where he offered the gift in order to rid me of my phobia.

Well I did feel it became less of a trouble after, hmm? must be some kind of magic!

So we spent about five hours that day travelling up all the mountain from Baby to King to Mother Koli and its there that I paid more attention to the white granite stones which appeared to be quiet crystalline it is unique and the fact that its white granite rock makes it very special also.

And now I was noticing small pieces of small granite crystal rock on the path of which I chose three small pieces and then there was a bigger more crystal looking one the size of my hand and I had to have it!

On the descent we came across the hotel and we read the plaque on the wall that says Baby Koli was a place where maidens would take small gifts as a sacrifice when asking the spirits for a favour!

Daniel had not seen this nor did he know of it before taking my stone to the sacrifice place but I was getting used to his dimensional energy and Natalie confirmed that he was special in that way and I did feel that although I had not found shungite there were other gifts to be discovered here.

Ilka had told me of a friendly ghost story they encountered when first arriving to manage the place there as there were strange clicking noises and other worldly events occurring which after a time they forgot their fears and invited the spirits to live in harmony with them and I was ok with that story but the last night I was there he told me of a man who'd committed suicide and how someone had drowned in the well which is why it was closed and padlocked.

That evening l saw a man who wasn't not there wearing brown corduroy trousers which was a bit disconcerting and then that night I heard lots of clicking sounds and as I was on my own and outside the main house I felt quiet spooked so lit the lamp and did not sleep much.

Anyhow I did survive the night and Kai had made an amazing breakfast to go for me and then Lisa kindly drove me to the coach stop where we hugged goodbye.

Magic Stories

It was a good coach ride with a very pleasant driver and back in Helsinki I reconnected with Outi who had arranged for me to house and cat sit a colleagues flat in the city and I was relieved to have a place to stay.

Of the two cats living in the flat one was the skinniest cat I had ever seen and one was the fattest and incontinent Urgh and no access to a garden but beggars can't be choosers and I was still really grateful so I fed the cats and escaped daily to Soumenlinna where as the weather was good I swam and wrote the complete story of the soldier.

The stones there continued to pour out this story for me and as it weaved its way into my conciousness a new kind of story teller was being born inside of me and was beginning to hold me in a timeless magic place.

I was truly in a state of bliss and renamed the island, "The Land of the Story Telling Stones".

Then when the story was finished at some point I called it "The Sleeping Stars of Soumenlinna".

The magic continued, as I stood at the shoreline on the little beach a small branch floated up to the shore and my newly attuned story telling eyes saw it was special and my story telling ears heard the branch say.

"Hello I am your next story, I am the King of the Elves and I've been on a mission around this world but if you take me home with you then I will tell you the story" Well! Of Course I did just that.

Meanwhile there was the August food festival so it was yum yum time and I took my cards and handed them out to stall holders and I received a few very generous responses.

Story Telling Day

This time every year there is a day called Story Telling Day which is like a sort of organic festival occasion where stories are told and funky things happen and I wanted to read my story on the island to someone as I was on a mission to honour all the soldiers who remained on Soumenlinna.

Delia the flat holder was back home and I read her the soldier story and having enjoyed it she tasked me with finding another magic story that day, so I went to Soumenlinna and swam as usual and I was just sunbathing when I caught sight of a young man standing at the edge of the sea holding a huge bunch of tansy in front of his face. "What's your story" I called to him before he wandered away. "Follow me" he said and Yargo was his name and so I did.

We arrived at a big smooth rock where a beautiful woman was draped over it. "What is your story" I asked her and she said that she had slept outside in a hammock for ten nights so I read her my poem.

I asked if I could read her my story of The Sleeping Stars to which she consented to, so I told the story and as I did so l became aware of an audience arriving of six or so folk and when I had finished.

I asked the tansy boy Yargo to have tea with me and he thanked me but said it was a hectic day and there was a meeting and after a while I realised that he was part of this theatrical group!

Yargo was born on one of the islands and was I believe one of life's truly gentle souls and though I would have liked to have tea with him one day.

It has yet to happen and I felt I had by relating the soldier story honoured the spirit of the soldiers who could not leave.

Well that was the magic story I took back to Delia and she enjoyed it.

I filmed a big protest march there, the first of its kind against austerity and bad politics, what to say about it? Well it was quiet merry with a samba band as it snaked through the city and over a bridge.

Then I met with Kiara and Frida and we bought two copies of the Kalevala for gifts.

Sami Parliment

I decided to travel to Inari again to give some cards to the Sami at the museum there and also to revisit Wolfgang at the Arctic Circle so I booked an overnight train and left Helsinki.

I decided to travel straight to Inari first and then drop by at the Arctic Circle on the way back.

This time in Inari I got off the coach stop outside of the camp site and I had taken my tent to camp there this time which was a foolish move because although some how I managed to put it together it rained!

So I ended up in the cabin again and the weather was cold so no swimming this time and worse, there was no blue berries cos the weather was too cold Urghh.

But I spent more time at the Sami museum this time and gave them some cards as a gift then I realised that the big wooden building close by was the Sami Parliament which is a very big long but slightly rounded wooden structure.

I went inside and glad I did for it was indeed beautiful and sensitively fashioned in natural materials with rounded walls and a tourist shop that played spell binding Sami music that did not lose the magic for the inclusion of musical instruments.

I bought a CD of one of the singers for my daughter Indra I looked into the debating room which was also big on wood in fact the whole of this place was a pleasure to be inside of it.

Sami Sacred Island

I also this time took a hover boat with a new friend Mariana from Switzerland to the Sami Sacred Island the lake we travelled over was the same lake outside my camping place and it is huge!

The Sami sacred island was like a very small mountain of rocks and small trees with wooden stairs leading up to the top and we passed by a small Sami burial island on the way.

Though the sacred island did feel magical I couldn't walk to the top on the wooden steps so accepted some kind person's hand to hold to get down from about the middle of it.

Mariana told me about a walk to the Sami church "Only one hour" she said.

So the next day I did walk to it and there was the initial two miles to get to the car park and then two hours of walking carefully on a path littered with tree roots and stones.

About half an hour in there, by a clear lake was a traveller's rest place complete with outside fire a big wooden shelter a compost loo and a shed load of wood!

How cool was that! And there I met a young shy couple from Cheque Republic who like walking in remote areas and we walked together the rest of the way.

This forest really blew me away as it was more rugged than the first Troll Forest and dominated by huge rocks that did look very much alive to my eyes and so did the smaller smoother ones and I confirmed quietly to myself that I would not enjoy walking there in the dark.

At last we arrived at the Sami Church area to find a great log sleeping cabin with a traditional Sami chimney of stones there was a great outdoor fire place and the usual compost loo and shed of fire wood and also a smoke sauna cabin.

Three Pagan Girls

And sitting at the fire place were three young women whom I quickly identified as pure Pagan and their energy was truly magical Rikka, Kaisa and Milla.

Their stories were that they were all studying Sami crafts at the school there and they were sleeping in the log cabin for a while and I learned that they had sung and chanted with some well known Sami musicians.

We passed a most pleasant afternoon and I swam in the lake there.

The church was wooden and simple and I did not like it at all because I know that the Sami were originally Pagan and would only drop their religion under extreme duress.

This area was the winter camping place for the reindeer travelling Sami and that I liked a lot there was a very big grass heart centre to the area which I am sure held amazing magic energies but I have not explored that yet and all this was surrounded by birch and pine trees and then a big clear lake to the left of the open fire. I wanted to stay with the girls but I was not prepared so I walked back through the forest before dark as I did not want to face a waking Troll at Twilight!

It is useful here to state that there was only one path to follow which was marked by a red plastic guide tape and all the way there were small roots and stones on the path which meant that a walker needed to be very concious of their steps and any leaving the path would lead to no other paths.

The journey felt like forever but after five hours of walking at last I was back at the camp site but I did return the next day and met the girls walking out of the forest so I shared food with them and planned to see them later.

I walked on and at the camp site I met some Russian men at the fire place who were on a works holiday with the biggest bread making company in Finland.

I was kindly offered a sausage I could not refuse and when I asked if the grain was organically grown the answer from the boss woman was that they care about the environment.

When they had left I again had a quick swim in the beautiful clear lake and then hurriedly set off again back through the forest as did I already say that I did not want to cross a Trolls path in the Twilight. I walked so much that day I lost weight and I was exhausted.

Santa Clause

Next day I took the bus to Roveniemi and then a short ride to the Arctic Circle where I went straight to Wolfgang's Top shop...

Where we exchanged an affectionate greeting and then I rather tentatively handed him the poem and picture of the Northern Lights.

He carefully looked at the poem and picture on my card and then looked at me with a friendly gleam in his eye "It's smooth" he said. Well that did mean a lot to me cos I had respect for this Crystal Man.

He then gave me lunch and four cups of coffee and we talked for ages where I shared some of my adventures with him and about my journey with shungit and I showed him the shungite crystal I had.

The holding pin had come apart which he then placed in a small metal cage that's safe to this day and then he spoke more about his love of the North and the Northern Lights which made a picture of him in my mind of a big friendly snow bear.

I did ask this time if I could visit Santa Clause when I realised that he was home Wolfgang kindly lead me all the way through the big magic structure past the big pendulum of time, which is where Santa borrows time from the world to give himself all the time he needs in which to deliver the presents on Christmas Eve.

It made perfect sense to me!

Then Wolfgang spoke to Santa quietly before leaving me there and I was invited as any child would be to sit next to the Santa Clause whilst he asked me some kindly questions about my journey.

Santa's room was quiet big with a warm atmosphere and Xmas maps on the wall and he himself was not big and very round but tall with a red hat, white shirt, red waistcoat and an apron and of course a long white beard.

It had been a very long time since I last visited Santa Clause but my inner child knew how to handle the event and Santa was so friendly that all of me was at ease.

But my inner child was also in a state of awe to meet this one great Magic Being who traditionally loves all children and understands the innocent and joyous nature of them and of course he makes it a life's mission to support the importance of wonder and magic playtime and presents.

I told him about the Northern Lights experience and I liked his magic energy which was clearly visible to see.

When I left and was in the main foyer I saw me with Santa on a big tv screen!

That was a huge surprise and I was given the code to download the video of it and some stills.

I expect children are thrilled by all that, I certainly was really pleased with the experience and my family were given unusual Xmas cards that year!

Wolfgang in a playful mood, teased me with a game where anything I wanted was only five euros but it took a long time for me to realise and I was not left with enough time to visit the Sami boy Yoonas, but he is a face book friend so I knew could message him.

I bought some raw amber and then he gave me a lift to my chaga tree next to the river and with a big hug he was gone.

I gathered some chaga and then walked to the train station.

On arriving in Helsinki I found Frida and gave her the tent and all things relating to it. The relief I felt at ridding myself of the tent was immeasurable! For the burden of it as I did realise by now that though the trolley looks cool in UK, in Finland l just looked like a homeless refugee. DOH!

Then after a while it dawned on me that I was a day too early with no where to stay so I sat in Mcdonalds for an hour or so in the evening with a mint tea.

After a while I was dealing with an aggressive security thug who shouted at me when I closed my eyes, so l gave that up and visited the metal pub for a while, which was so much nicer.

Then I ended up at the airport for the night which was ok and comfortable.

In the morning I chose to take the train option back to Helsinki which meant taking an escalator down through densely carved out granite stone.

The first ride down was challenging enough but when it was followed by some more downward moving stairs my other phobia for spacial depth got triggered as this place reminded me of the Mines of Moria from Lord of the Rings where Gandalf said they had dug too deep and awoken the Dark Ancient Demon far below which I was expecting to appear in my imagination at any moment soon.

But I did survive the trauma which made greeting the out door sun so much sweeter then I took the ferry to Soumenlinna said a sad farewell to the Island of Story Telling Stones after a swim and a cold shower on the edge of the Half Moon sandy beach and then watched the foam dance around the brow of the boat on the way back to Helsinki mainland. In the beginning uncertainty of where to stay I was feeling vulnerable so I had shortened my visit to the 5th of September by a few days I regretted now as I just needed a bit more faith to stay longer.

A Leap of Faith

Then later when I took the plane home and I put the stick Id found at Soumenlinna beach on my big window ledge next to the big white granite crystal from Mother Koli mountain in Karelia.

With not a clue where or what or even If the story would arrive but in keeping with the magic nature of storytelling I had to trust the invisible and allow that when the time came then the story would arrive! That's a huge leap of faith.

So l went foraging and for five weeks that is all l was doing and did not put my attention on writing stories.

After foraging was over with berries gathered and potions made l sat down and then my patience and faith bore fruit as the story arrived and unravelled itself in a most surprising way.

Writing Faery Tales can put me right in the timeless magic zone and it is the best drug I have ever known and this story flowed effortlessly and brought a new delight every day.

Erkel Derkel Elf

The second story was about Nature and Erkel Derkel the Elf and the subject was saving trees and all their magic and all sorts of other magic and oh yes a little Sami girl that I called Eleena I called it, "I Am Gone with Stick".

I thought that was it! after writing the two stories but I was just sitting again one day and something strange happened in the form of some Trolls who appeared out of the Soumenlinna of my imagination and at first I ignored them cos they really had a putrid smell which did not appeal to me at all but they absolutely would not go away so I just gave up trying to ignore them and surrendered to the story and so glad I did cos it was really great fun to write and helped open doors for the future of all the magical characters. And I named that "The Troll Collective".

I made little printed books of the three stories. Which became Xmas presents for family and friends.

Painted Goddess Puzzle

I turned my focus now to the task of painting the dancing Goddesses which carried a lot of logistics as I wanted to get as close to the original drawings as possible but I somehow managed to create twelve paintings on 12/16 inch canvases that looked ok to my eyes but lacked the flowing serpent movement hmm?!

Not all solutions arrive at once but one day I woke up to a vision of Northern Lights dancing Goddesses on a big round puzzle!

It had to be and now my focus was sharp to it.

I enlisted the help of a friend who easily cut the puzzle pieces from a large piece of ply wood with an electric saw and I worked from there painting it till l was satisfied but I had not for seen how to frame 4ft/4ft puzzle with 16 interlocking pieces.

A small anomaly occurred where one piece of the interlocking puzzle was very narrow and broke under the strain of fitting with its partner piece

I had also applied for an artist residency on Soumenlinna but was refused as too many applications and I was not professional but I was not daunted and continued with the art project anyway.

Great Expectations

There is a balance l try and hold between the creative process, logistic problem solving and ambition and I realise after the event that ambition dominated the creative process and in this influence I decided to take all my art back to Helsinki and find a commission to paint another Northern Lights puzzle wheel.

I was so confident of success that I did not buy a return ticket home! (Well, what could possibly go wrong?)

I had become used to seeking the advice of my psychic medium friend Maxine Temple on matters of making practical moves with my art projects and I sought her advise a bit late in the day now for this adventure.

I had a great invitation to stay at a friends place in Helsinki but an unexpected event cancelled it so I was looking at an uncertain future again.

"The Spirits are telling me that you are not ready yet to go on your journey and they are concerned that you don't have a place to stay" she said "I've bought the ticket" I replied stubbornly and I was determined to go regardless of problems.

I quietly asked my Ancestors for assistance and let the matter rest with them and I had an address from a person of a place I could show my paintings in Helsinki before I left and I was certain that I could place the magic stories.

You Know The Way

I saw a four wheeled trolley suitcase Australian make and 34 inches tall

"Just big enough to take all the paintings and other art materials" l told myself and of course another trolley case for stuff.

I messaged Outi about my problem of nowhere to stay and she responded with these words "You know the Way" which gave me time out from a huge problem and I felt grateful to have such a great friend.

I decided also to see the Summer Solstice in Finland so l booked a flight for 14th of June.

Bad planning made for penalty fee for over weight at the air port and a sleepless night there sorting it all out.

I arrived in Helsinki on a great summer day really tired.

Remarkably it all turned out good as I was left in charge of Outi's two Gerbils for a month whilst she and her family were away on holiday but not before I sat with the family and watched Iceland beat England in the world cup football which was an interesting surreal moment.

This was the first time I was secure for the duration in a home and I felt grateful for that and I lost no time in visiting the café where there was a possibility showing my art but the place was closing for holidays and other places I took the stories to were not interested so I really quickly gave up and decided that I got it wrong and the Finnish way was not the same as my dream so I Let It Go!

The broken piece of the picture puzzle was glued and then broke again so I had brought it to Finland along with the glue to mend it.

Whilst calling my friend Annabell in the UK I mentioned the broken puzzle piece and then I told her about a dream I had years ago with a missing puzzle piece and I did so because since I did get the idea to paint a picture as a puzzle the memory of that dream began to subtly emerge but I had no in-depth understanding only that I did regard my life somewhat as a puzzle.

In my dream there was my estranged father standing with his back to me just inside the doorway of another room where he had put together a huge puzzle that was on a table but there was a piece missing and it was the last piece.

He then turned around to face me saying these words.

"Here now you finish it"

Some dreams feature big in the memory and this one I never did forget.

(Some significance that I had brought the puzzle to Finland with a piece missing)

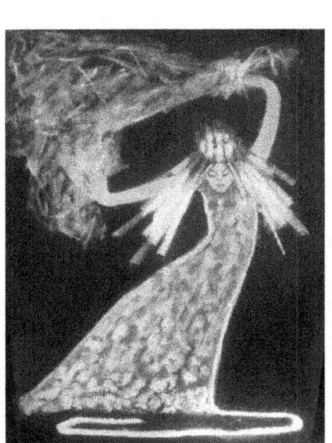
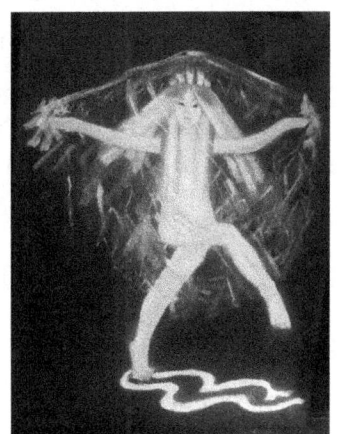

Majestic Clouds

After a big faff the broken piece was glued fast and I just fixed it and disappeared out the door to continue my adventure.

I visited the metal pub only to find it was no more and that was a really sad thing for me to lose the oasis of friendly metal folk and when I return to Helsinki I will make it a mission to find another.

I visited Soumenlinna asap and it was great to be there again and the summer was really warm with clear skies this year.

Ducks were many also mummy ducks with chicks that took a lot of my attention as their lives seemed to be precariously balanced between safe and tragic with two mummy ducks and various chicks that would be there one day and gone the next leaving eventually I baby chick with one mummy duck that was once four and three remaining chicks from the other mummy ducks five.

I did my best to feed them from my pastries and they had no fear of me so that was the easy part all the rest of the dramas about their survival did my head in.

I discovered that there was a very low salt content in the ocean making it possible for the ducks to drink from it and I did not want to dwell to much on the missing chicks as it was depressing enough to witness the apparent lack of care for wild life on the beach with boys throwing things at them and when I did talk about it with a rare animal rights campaigner she said it was a cultural thing which made me sad but it did cause me to feel relieved that in the UK we culturally are very passionate about wild life and protecting it.

I tried to find the girl who had given me the paper to write stories on the previous year but I don't think she was there so l gave the stories to someone there and this became a pattern where l would at times gift someone with the three stories and ask them to email their response to them.

On that trip I gave away 90 stories mostly to strangers.

My camera had got broken in flight so I had my I phone only now to rely on for pictures.

This time of being in Finland was a different energy and I just was grateful to be under clear skies looking at real clouds indeed one day was just so magical when an army of big round clouds just floated gently across the sky all day and to my mind they took on heroic shapes of Angels and Warriors in my imagination and I spent a whole day enjoying them.

It had been perhaps 15 years since I had seen such beautiful plump pink clouds.

I was also watching the energy of the foaming water dancing over the brow of the ferry each time I travelled on it to Soumenlinna which was another inspiration.

I used the metro on a part of my journey and one day I came across some Hari Krishna devotees playing and chanting so I sat down and enjoyed the music and the spiritual energy that it invoked.

I encountered them several times there over some days then something occurred in that place with them that I found truly shocking!

I arrived at the metro one day to a dramatic scene where a large ugly woman was shrieking abuse in English at the Krishnas on a microphone attached to a loud speaker and amid the insults I was able to pick out accusations of devil worship! Another big ugly woman was filming this Ogress obviously to show it off somewhere publicly.

I felt compelled to do something so I rushed over to the Lush shop nearby and asked them to call the police who did arrive ten minutes later and the scene changed with the Ogress being moved on.

Throughout the whole time of this tirade a female Krishna devotee was gently dancing to the music and chanting along with all the rest which I thought was a testimony to her courage and unbreakable faith. (Hari Krishna)

There are many Krishna devotees in the UK who receive a lot of respect as they do freely feed many people and they are a colourful site at music festivals.

Indeed my long time Krishna friend Jamuna is still making and feeding folk for free in Glastonbury and was a very welcome sight feeding the eco warriors up on Sacred Solsbury Hill some 20 odd years ago where he stayed till the bitter end with us all protecting it. I recall one terrible day when the last tree had been killed in the water meadow and the landscape seemed to put out a black shadow in despair and we all were emotionally traumatised as we walked a very long and weary way up the hill.

Where we were greeted by Jamuna waiting with a kind heart and hot food and it was medicine for our aching hearts and souls and I remembered all that when I encountered the Krishna folk because they all do this thing of feeding people.

Sami Shaman on the Metro

Around this time frame in the metro I saw Eleena, a woman in her thirties with cropped hair preaching some thing to the hurrying crowds that passed her by and she caught my interest and so I approached her and asked what her story was.

She was friendly toward me and said she had been to India and became a Buddhist Nun "Why return?" I enquired. Her answer was intriguing and I listened intently as she unravelled her story. Her father was a Sami Shaman and she returned home to Finland because of a conflict of spiritual cultures and yet she was preaching about the evils of materialism in quiet a Buddhist way.

She said that when the police witness her doing this then they threaten her with arrest.

As she was talking to me some thing remarkable occurred as we both connected on a really deep spiritual level where I felt safe enough to drop all my protective barriers till we became united souls, which startled her a little I think but also pleased her.

Her father was a Sami Shaman married to an unbeliever which eventually broke his heart and so he took himself and his drum to a tree and hung himself.

The more she spoke the more I experienced the quality of her energy and I was getting impressions now of her heart energy which she said was open and she could not shut it down so I guess that she puts all her heart energy into trying to wake people up.

I noticed she had a bottle of white wine in a paper bag which she was sipping and after questioning her about that it became clear that it was to dull the emotional pain of people not listening.

I wanted to spend more time with her but she wanted to go up to the street and preach again so I followed her but kept a distance and then I reluctantly left as I was wanting to talk and she chose another path.

This meeting haunted me and I reflected deeply on all the aspects of her heart energy which I recall was open devotional and constant till I felt that Eleena actually held the spirit of her father as she probably inherited the gift of Shamanism from him which meant she embodied the very soul memories of the Sami people just as a Shaman would do and also the heart of them. Albeit it a bit broken.

This is the energy that so enchanted me that I had searched for in every Sami person in Inari that I had met but not found.

And here it was this year in Helsinki right in my world offered as a gift in answer to my need to connect with the conciousness of this Sami Indigenous tribe of people that I have such a deep respect for.

It pained me now to know that I was not quick witted enough to impart this belief to her and I tried to find her again with no success.

A strange small thing occurred to me after a time the name I gave to the little Sami girl in my Elf story was Eleena and I had not heard this name before nor did I research this as an appropriate Sami name indeed I can't say why I chose it to this day! So I must leave her for now and hope that we can reunite next time.

I was preoccupied with the need to find the two navel officers again to give them some stories but that proved more of a mission than I imagined.

I was able to talk with a young good looking cadet just doing his national service for some months and I told him the story of how I met the two navel officers and gave him some stories with a request that he try and deliver them to Lt. Juhana and Cpt. Elleryelf and that is all I could do.

There is a saying in Finland apparently that clever men join the air force and good looking men join the navy hmm interesting.

I asked about the short hair rule for short term national service recruits and the answer was there are no exceptions.

My interest was due to having a Finnish fb friend who lives in Norway and he has the most amazingly beautiful long blonde hair right down to his knees which will not just grow back soon after being severely cut in the months of national service and a boys long hair is vital part of his identity and losing it I believe would be truly depressing and I really sympathise with him.

Solstice on Soumenlinna

Midsummer in Finland is the nearest weekend to the Summere Solstice and on that day its a bit like Xmas where the buses stop and many folk travel to their own small island to celebrate or if you re left in the city then you can at a price visit small islands on a boat and look at other folks celebration fires.

Pagan Summer Solstice is usually 20 to 21st of June and I had planned to stay up all Solstice night to watch the dawn on Soumenlinna Island which l did and as the setting sun was over the ferry port facing away from Helsinki then I placed my self just there all night apart from a few short walks and it is an endurance which ever way its looked at but l just wanted to do this.

The sun did not quiet set being so far north and the sky remained light tinged with yellow and there are sea gulls on the island that just did not go to sleep and made a din screeching all night long.

When it was really early morning the sun was a bright red ruby nestling on the surface of the sea whilst its mirror image was pouring out over the bay, Perfection!

I took the first morning ferry back to Outi's and slept a while but as the nights were so light and the days were so long it altered my sleep patterns and I was awake very late usually.

I met a woman in her garden on my way to the story telling stones on the other end of the island she lived in one of the big granite housing block.

I gave her three stories and a few days later she connected with me and gave me a gift of a Finnish designed cup in response as a thank you which I was touched by and we travelled on the ferry and I discovered that her father had been a fisherman and they had lived on one of the small islands.

I saw her a few times and I have her address and l appreciated her warmth as I was finding out this time to Helsinki that Fins are not very communicative and before whilst giving away poems and art I was getting a false impression of their willingness to communicate.

The Ateneum this year did not inspire me as I did not like the modern artist showcased but it was still a refuge for me so I d go and sit and use the Wi-Fi and on a particular day I ordered a pot of tea "Where is the tea from" I enquired "India" was the answer and I realised that as Finns drink mostly coffee they don't understand the subject and the tea I had there was woeful but I enjoyed the honey that came with it.

I remembered Megan took me for a birthday treat to the fisherman's cafe on the beach in the seaside town I grew up in where a pot of tea for one was big enough for four people and had four tea bags inside with one extra on the side (just in case you wanted it stronger!)

The whole tea culture is an English tradition that I treasure simply because we understand the flavour of different teas and we know how to brew it and we understand also the nurturing aspect of it.

Indeed some people make a nice cup of tea for a guest with all the care and ceremony of a tea maker in an ancient tea ceremony. Hot sweet tea is also used to help with shock.

Jerry and the Moika Fish

A good thing happened where I saw small fish on a fish stall at the market that looked good and as I would not buy meat I looked on it as my protein source and wow it was good just dusted in flour and fried in coconut oil and they are called moika or wendies and live in the deep fresh water lakes and are cousin to salmon.

I connected with Jerri who works on the fish stall and we became fb friends.

And he told me that he mostly goes away to Asia in winter to avoid the depression and I expect judging by the fb pics that he also has a great time and as he loved metal music he advised me on some good bands and helped broaden my metal music horizons.

TUSKA

There is a metal music festival in Helsinki each year called Tuska (which means agony!) situated in Kalasatema anyway the tickets were sold out on line so as it was on my metro route I popped in on the Friday to beg to buy a Sunday ticket and stood in a queue to do this.

Then a young man asked why I was queuing and said that I could get in free "WHY" I asked and the answer was that people over sixty go free to Tuska! Well how chuffed was I (totally mind blown) sooo!

I didn't have my pass port or other Id proof of age but I happen to have my bus pass in my wallet so I showed it to the security at the gate and I can now say that I got in to a metal music festival with my bus pass!

The delicious obscurity of this event was not wasted because this is a story that will run through out the rest of my life and I hope to hear my grandchildren tell their children about the day that Great Nana got in to a metal music festival with her bus pass!

Well ok I'm in and what do I see? hmm, the venue is an old disused power station with a big round chimney and smaller buildings one large marquee one indoor stage and one big main stage some grass area for chilling the usual fast food stalls and as I discovered later a smoke sauna tent that was free.!

The bands were really good and throughout the festival I was able to add about ten new band names to my like list and there was one name of Gojira that Jerri had given me.

Ear plugs were sold as there was not the space and distance to dissipate the sound and crowd surfing was taboo as the stage area was on tarmac but I bore that disappointment with a good heart and just really enjoyed the experience.

This place Helsinki is the home of my music band Wintersun and they would have played at Tuska so I felt I was on Sacred Ground.

Smoke Sauna Tent

The smoke sauna was held in a big army tent and it contained two big smoke wood burning stoves and three tiers of wooden benches arranged on two sides and outside was a place to leave the cast off clothes in the careful hands of lovely girls who gave out old large beer mats to sit on.

I sat on the lowest bench level near the stoves because I didn't want to get too hot and from this vantage point I saw close up each time there was water dribbled on the sauna stones.

A man very quietly would enter the sauna tent about every five minutes and gather water from a wooden bucket with a long handled wooden ladle and then with all the expertise of a master craftsman would gently pour just enough water on the stones on top of the wood burner to make it sizzle and smoke.

The Fins do sauna so well and its one thing about their culture that's to love

This action of the water pouring awakened some deep past memory and placed me in an ancient zone and the water pouring took on a whole spiritual Pagan ceremony and I was enthralled by it all!

It did not matter that this ex army tent was not a 100 year old smoke sauna like my experience in Karelia as it lost none of the magic ceremony and atmosphere and I was just as comfortable. (The Finns do the Sauna so masterfully well)

There were naked men arriving constantly and unusually talking a lot and then a man found the wooden bucket with water and birch twigs which he began to beat his body with which I discovered helped with the whole sauna process.

I braved a cold water tap after my sauna experience and I did return the next day where the experience was still a magic one.

Amazing Metal Bands

There was a band called Primordial and the lead singer was Irish and it all just sounded so hauntingly beautiful and very deep and I made a note to hear more of this band later at home on line and later I did that.

The Irish group Primordial that I found to be so haunting have a music genre of Celtic metal Pagan Doom and Black Metal and have I believe a strong grasp of the past and I searched some songs and found The Coffin Ships which is sung by Alan Averill about the Irish Famine and there is a song called The Ghosts of Charnel House that's about child abuse from the past.

These subjects are all played and sung from the heart with complete sincerity and that's probably why I found it to be hauntingly beautiful.

I'd missed Lordi as they played early on Friday but saw and enjoyed many other bands.

I bought my musical son Mathew a floppy beer cooler with the word Tuska printed on it for his soon to be birthday and some small things and also a T shirt that denoted the year 2016 and Tuska printed on it with names of the bands very cool I thought.

There was no place to camp here so fans just went home later on the late bus about 11 pm.

The last day I was at the festival I wore a green lacy long dress that prompted a woman to hug me saying that I reminded her of her grandmother who presumably was a hippie once. "I'm not hugging you just cos I'm drunk" she assured me first and I accepted this experience and returned the affectionate hug.

And I met there an interesting man who took photos of the bands and said he knew Jari Maenpaa and I met him again going my way on the late night bus and we talked a little more I was so wanting to meet my musical god Jari but did not want to be too gushing so I just gave him a poem with a request to pass it on to him and he did say that Jari was working on some new music.

Bad Hair Day

"After the excitement of Tuska there did not seem to be anything else going on" I wrote in my diary.

Just a few random events like four brilliant violinists playing on the city streets to inspire me and then one evening.

I was going home when my attention was taken by some really good metal music sounds which I followed and it lead me to a side street where tickets were being sold for an outdoor concert.

Out of nowhere some security guard was shouting at me not in English so I made it known to him that I was from the UK which did not sink in with him and he roughly pushed me and though I was in a state of shock I jumped back at him with a long and loud lecture about economy and tourists and his disgraceful behaviour which was embellished with a liberal use of the F word.

I complained about the incident to two good looking policemen nearby and one of them asked "What do you want me to do about it?" "Tell him off" I said but his response was that he could not do anything from his police car and I should go to some police station to make a complaint!

If that cop had said to me that he wasn't able to do anything because he was having a bad hair day it would have made as much sense and that day marked a big change in my relationship with the Finnish public as the cracks in their society were just getting bigger for me and I was fast falling out of love with them.

I visited the island of Haraka that Id gone to on my first visit to give the stone artist woman some stories but she wasn't there so I gave the stories to an English man who was the caretaker there and chatted for awhile and I related the security guard incident to him and learned more about how limited the police powers were.

One of the reasons I was concerned was that at the moment of the policeman not being able to do anything the security guard who may have not even have been Finnish and a total thug also had more power than all the laws in Finland.

I did not want to be cynical but the step from melancholia which is what I d sunk into cynicism was not a pleasant or difficult one.

Then I learnt that I had missed the farewell gig of Black Sabbath. (No Words)

Chinese Moxibustion ST36

Before leaving the island I walked a little and then I was bitten on my hand by probably a midge which swelled up and so I went to the health store and bought Apis Mel which is a homoeopathic remedy for allergic reactions.

I phoned my twin sister in UK who is good with healing stuff and she assured me I would live but it would take a while to get better and I was feeling really vulnerable as I had no confidence to go to hospital now and I was thinking to return to UK but I had taken with me some Chinese moxibustion sticks and I remembered my acupuncturist Selena tell me about a powerful acupuncture point named stomach 36 just below the knee so I moxered it and the next morning the swelling had gone right down which raised my confidence level and though there were other bites I was able to cope with them.

"Character building" I told Outi whilst recounting the experience when she returned home some days later.

Meeting Teemu Mäntysaari on Metro

Not a lot happened for days but then it was the 20th of July my son Mathew's birthday and the floppy bear cooler had reached him ok and I was on my way to Soumenlinna on the metro and something happened and in my diary I called it "Something Mad and Magic".

I was sitting on a metro seat and then I looked up and sitting opposite me was a good looking man who d just sat down and it was Teemu Mäntysaari of Wintersun my favourite metal music band Wintersun and the reason I had travelled all the way to Finland because their music totally zapped me with ancient elemental energy and visions that recalibrated my spiritual compass, YES THAT ONE! and the rhythm guitarist was sitting opposite me on the metro!

I had to speak or fade away forever so I said his name "Teemu Mäntysaari" and then as calmly as I could manage enquired on the good health of Jari Mäenpää and the gist of it was that I remembered that he gave guitar lessons so I asked for one and he booked me in for a few days time.

WOW I phoned Megan asap and asked how I should be with him.

"Nana don't give him too much work" she said and I think she meant not to talk too much as she knows me quiet well. Then I phoned Morgana who had a different aspect to offer.

"Wow Nana what are the chances to meet him like that and you've got to tell him everything about how you feel because this will never happen again."

I'm very blessed to have such wise and passionate grand daughters and after I reflected on their advice I decided to take a little from each of them to be open and brave but not too gushing.

I borrowed an acoustic guitar and practised to strengthen my fingers as I had not played for years.

I was feeling quiet anxious about the lesson but decided that just having the experience of spending time with my music hero was worth a lot.

The day arrived and I realised that I had become quiet melancholic over the weeks in Helsinki but I wanted to be my best for this special event and was preoccupied with this dilemma as I took the metro to Kalasatema which is where Teemu teaches guitar at the Sonic Pump Studio.

Unforgetable Guitar Lesson with Teemu Mäntysaari

I had to negotiate the strange architecture of the metro station as it triggers my phobia of heights due to the station being high up with lots of glass walls but as I had overcome my elevator problem I was a bit more hopeful of dealing with this.

I needed assistance to go up in the at the Sonic Pump studio lift and then I was there waiting for a short while outside Teemu's studio and when he bid me welcome it was with such a warmth that a lot of my nerves disappeared.

His studio was comfortable with many electric guitars neatly hanging up a huge computer screen a sofa a comfy student chair and his seat.

Something came up about my name and he said he knew as he found it on line because he kept the magic story book that I d handed him at the Summer breeze festival the first time I saw them live.

I was speechless with amazement and deeply moved that he would do such a thing and it showed such a generous nature and a quality of respect that is rare in the Mainstream music scene but maybe this was another clue about metal being family.

I did tell him that the Music of Wintersun took me to Finland and something about how I felt but I don't remember much what I said that day.

I remembered more of what he said but I was glad to say it all and then he gave me a plectrum with a Wintersun logo on it and I was thrilled with that as it sealed a teacher student relationship and I felt that was a nice touch and a great way to begin the lesson.

He showed me about five things to play and I was so very impressed with his teaching skills as it became clear that he was a natural teacher and that is a rare quality.

His energy gave me the impression of a green and blue balance which mean to me natural teacher and healer and it was just such a difference from the energy of the many dark looks I d got on this my third journey to Helsinki and it was so very healing to experience it.

After a while he invited me to jam a little with him and I chose the Leonard Cohen song of Marianne as I used to play it a lot with my son Mathew and it was safe and familiar so he found the song on line very fast and played rhythm to my musical fumblings in such a beautiful easy way that I was convinced that this Demi God of music could play anything at all and he gently showed me a way to play a cord in a more coherent way.

As an afterthought now England lost some great legends later that year and though Leonard Cohen was Canadian he was an important musician in my life and I find it a bitter sweet tribute to him that my new music hero and I played a little of his iconic song and it means a lot to me now.

Then after an hour when the lesson was over he asked to take a photo of us both as he does that with his students so wow! how cool that was to be. He then showed me around the whole studio and even the room where Wintersun recorded Time I and to me, and I am sure to all other Wintersun fans, this studio is Hallowed Ground.

We talked a bit about the crowd funding to build a Wintersun studio and he showed me all the pictures on the walls of successful metal musicians but as yet there were no photos of Wintertsun there and I so wanted to see Wintersun there but more records needed to be sold and I felt quiet fiercely loyal in my resolve to help make that happen. I do remember telling Teemu that I wanted to see Wintersun play at Glastonbury Festival as I knew they d be totally adored.

I took a few photos of the studio and Teeemu and then I asked him to take the lift with me so he accompanied me down and gave me a gentle hug goodbye at the exit door.

And so at last I had met with one of my Musical Heroes MAGIC.

That was a life changing moment for me as it lifted my spirits and also made me feel confidant in learning to play the electric guitar.

Indeed the whole experience of meeting by chance on the metro and the guitar lesson was a huge Magic Moment that I will never forget.

Then my inspiration returned and I felt honoured that he would give all that time to me.

I booked a ferry to Estonia for the day and I realised that I really love to travel in this way its relaxing and I was loving to see when the sun shines on the sea how it becomes a big diamond jewel.

Estonia was quaint with lovely old houses and I discovered linen there in forms I had not seen before and I bought Megan a knitted linen shawl and socks for Mog with reindeer on them and a knitted woollen shawl for my daughter Indra.

I was told by a new friend sharing Outi's house that she saw woman washing large linen sheets in the river which didn't make sense until I read a linen label that said avoid washing machine as linen will have a much longer life as hand washed.

I also now was planning to leave by boat to Sweden and then across to Denmark.

Age is just a Number Right?!

I emailed Teemu to say how the magic was returned to me and that I thought some people are natural teachers and some are natural healers and I believed that he had both the qualities and I sent him a long email about how the lesson went and he sent me a link to his fb page so I looked and saw the photo of him and me!

He looked beautiful but my initial reaction to being out there on the web was something beginning with AAAGH!

But I soon calmed down because it was all part of the magic and a privilege to be on da web wid ma hero.

The words Teemu wrote along with the photo began with the words

"Age is just a number right"? And some kind words about me being an artist and having as much passion for metal music as the young folk and also I was his oldest student! And that quiet blew me away as being a writer I am always appreciative when I see clever and inspired prose.

Mad and Magic!

There was more to my posted words and more to his but there is a link to his site where it can be seen in full where he has an obvious skill with a camera and is well worth finding cos one can follow the musical journey of the Wintersun band.

Recently they have announced their newly recorded album which is soon to be released and sold as part of a crowd funding package deal to raise funds for their music studio.

And there's a 20th anniversary at Tuska 2017 where Wintersun will play and that is one not to miss and I realised that if the plan A where I stayed in the city had happened then I don't think I would have met with Teemu on that metro

So I had to believe and trust that everything was going to a more cosmic plan than mine even my apparent lapse in mental cohesion played its part!

Outi arrived back from holiday and I was booked on a Viking line ferry to Stockholm.

Vision of the Sea Goddess

I had to go for one last day on Soumenlinna where it was windy so I chose a big smooth rock to lay on about 20ft high and on the side of the beach and there I stayed for some hours.

During that time something strange occurred in the sea just below and I could see that near the edge of the water and the stones there became a large patch of sea that was a mid to dark blue in contrast to the rest of the ocean that was a lighter blue and it shone like a jewel!

It was a mixture of smaller patches of blue as if they had been painted with an artists brush and on the edges where they all connected together were tiny brilliant gold stars gleaming and then after a while great long strands of a lighter bluey green arrived on top of the patch and they were all the same width and length just floating like mermaids hair.

A thought flowed through my mind that it was the Goddess just floating by and I just happened to be in the right place at the right time to see her and the thing is that I believed that I was seeing this with my human eyes and that everyone could see what I was seeing and it felt so normal and natural that l almost let it slip by without making a note.

I reflected on this event for some time after and then I realised that it must have been a vision but as I was not in a familiar Magic Zone I did not recognise it for some time and coincidently the place I saw this vision was the same beach that I wrote The Sleeping Stars of Soumenlinna on!

So "Was this a gift that I nearly let go by unacknowledged?"

When I think of it l could cry but I feel really grateful to know that the magic of Soumenlinna Island could tolerate my state of melancholia.

Outi Angel to the Rescue

It was time to leave Finland but I had to get the train to Tuurkuu as it was less expensive and though the buses run late there was a gap of two hours where I d be stranded and it all meant I had to spend the night in the city which was worrying me as I didn't want to be close to another security guard.

Outi Angel came to my rescue again and offered me a lift for early morning Phew! What a friend indeed. So apart from being an Angel her daytime job is being a successful green buissness woman.

We said goodbye at the train station and I was away on the train with a two hour journey to the ferry port.

I had often seen the Viking ferry either in port at Helsinki where it looked huge or just sailing away with waving people I was becoming one of the waving folk now.

Floating City to Stockholm

It was an exciting moment. Did I say boat? I meant floating city as it was multilevelled and it boasted about five different bar areas with childrens' activities including a little disco area.

The windows were huge and I stood at the side where the sun was shining on the sea and as we left Tuurkuu we sailed along a bay which was forested on either side and when we cleared this and entered the shipping lane we were followed by big rolling clouds like the ones I saw on Soumenlinna Island all the way to Stockholm and it was simply heavenly.

The Ferry sailed in between tiny green islands all the way and the sea gleamed like diamonds and I understood why people loved boat cruises because it was so relaxing and here was food to eat all you like 10 euro breakfast and 15 euro lunch and as I was to travel on a coach for a long time I decided to enjoy the food and five kinds of fish for protein needs.

Ten hours later we arrived in Stockholm in the evening where we were taken by a coach to bus station and I found the three hour wait was bearable.

Flixbus had two cheerful drivers and I slept quiet well then we were travelling over a land bridge to Denmark.

Copenhagen

We arrived in Copenhagen in the morning which was fine but negotiating two trolley cases over partially cobbled pavements was a nightmare but some how I found the hostel that Mog had booked for me and signed in.

Copenhagen was yet another cultural shock as I expected quaint streets and a slower pace of life but I did eventually happen upon some house boats on the inlet of the sea which I liked a lot.

Christania

My daughter had told me about a big hippie community called Christiania previously controlled by the German army before a group of hippies squatted it in1971 and that is where I wanted to get to so I took a bus and got off at a very decorated stone arch entrance.

I had synchronistically met a Danish man in Helsinki who visited there many times and told me how to get there.

The complex was huge and there were many buildings as well as green land and I found a big lake that was surrounded by trees and grass in the centre.

Meeting the Elders Odin and Loki

Where I ended up was right at the spot where the Elders hang out.

There were two Elders sitting on a low wall under an arch of flowers and I sat near one and soon gave him three magic stories which he glanced at and said "You are a magic person you can stay."

Well that pleased me a lot then I conversed with another Elder who was more talkative but neither of them told me their name so I called the first one Odin as he seemed to have a great calm presence and authority and the other I named Loki because he was more playful.

Both Odin and Loki had said that keeping Christiania protected had been a constant battle and I understood that although Danes are very cool folk perhaps the authorities in this case were not.

Loki told me that they had handed over the responsibility for protecting Christiania to the strongest young men but what was there to protect? This was my generation so I know we held universal love and spiritual freedom very highly and Christiania embodied these principles in how they lived as free spiritual beings and the manifestation of that freedom probably challenged the status quo which Land of Smiley People would invite an attempt to enforce authoritative control.

I asked if there was a book written and yes many actually so I pulled back from attempting that project.

There were many market-like stalls selling anything from hippie clothes to cigarette papers in fact everything you would expect to see at a festival and many, many city folk visited this place on a daily basis as it is a really free space and no doubt therapy from the big city.

In this Christiania I did feel very comfortable wearing my long colourful dresses indeed I received complements like when I was on a bus and was short of 10 cents for the fare and a woman was quick to give it to me "You look very beautiful" she said to me and I was bowled over by this cos I d got used to the scowls of folk in Helsinki and so I named Copenhagen the land of the Smiley People.

Loki was going to show me where the ferry was that goes to the Little Mermaid statue which is located by the sea so we walked along the sea inlet and then halfway there he asked why we were walking and I laughed cos he was so stoned that he forgot!

Little Mermaid

Well the boat was not there any more so I walked for about two hours to get there and she was worth the walk but lots of other tourists also thought so and I had to dive in and out of them to take clear photos of her.

I think she was made in bronze and looked quiet shy seated on top of two large smooth round stones and she was beautiful and really small.

This was a pilgrimage for me as Hans Christian Anderson is my Faery Tale hero so I took many photos and slithered perilously along the slimly beach stones in order to get a close up photo.

Then somehow took the right bus back to the hostel but stopping off on the way at the train station to buy a ticket to the island of Odense the birth place of Hans Anderson and the following morning I was there.

Hans Anderson Museum Odense

The landscape to O dense was mostly green and flat land with some deciduous trees and the main city looked like a monster invading this delicate ancient town with soulless blocks of concrete "Why" I asked a young man taking surveys.

"To keep up with the competition of growth" was the reply and I gave him my opinion about that as all I could see was this ancient historical town which relies on the tourist trade because of Hans Christian Andersons imagination was being suffocated by high rise concrete Ogres.

Poorly signed directions meant I spent ages trying to find the museum but when I entered the grounds I was pleased as it was set in a real big green garden with a small lake and there was a big toy Castle also and trees and an outdoor area for eating and chilling.

The front entrance had a big glass window and I followed the carpeted path to the inside which was his childhood home.

To my eyes the metal wood burning stove and the four poster bed tucked beside it was a charming peak into that era and as his father was a shoemaker there was appropriate evidence on a simple wooden table of leather apron and shoe lasts.

There was so much of his art projects and historical pictures that I realised that I was only just getting to know this amazing man who could create magic characters from when he was a small boy simply by cutting them out with a pair of scissors.

He was a great poet and artist and there are two rugs that bear the patterns of his designs in the weave and I saw portraits of him that showed he was a handsome man.

At a particular time the play castle in the large garden opened and an actor lead a troupe of children all dressed in Anderson's faery tale characters and they sang the familiar songs from my childhood like The Ugly Duckling, Thumbelina, The Emperor's New Clothes etc.

I was enthralled by this and my inner child was ecstatic. The Little Mermaid floated on the lake and Thumbelina floated on a leaf of course.

Wow what a day and then there was still time to visit his birthplace house and that was now lovely and quaint but it does not now show the abject poverty that he was born into and I could empathise with his ambitious drive to be successful after such a challenging beginning.

I stayed as long as I was able that day and took many pictures.

There was a stressful faff with the hostel as I only booked one night and they took a whole day before telling me about the overspill room in the cellar Hmm!

I visited Christiania twice more and I met a Greenlander sitting on a step drinking beer of which he offered me one of the cans and I accepted as I was already sitting next to him it seemed the polite thing to do.

He had an extraordinarily handsome face with black hair and startling deep blue eyes and we chatted for a while where he told me that in Greenland's past there was a great scarcity of woman there so the men would brew alcohol from anything they could find then pour it into a barrel which they strapped on to their backs and travelled to the mainland to trade it for a wife.

You could not make this up! and I think he said that his mother arrived in that way.

I was intrigued by his story and so let him do most of the talking, he said also that houses trap people's spirits in a sense that people become their house and he lives in a little nest that he fashioned for himself.

As we were talking the people passing by would drop money into an old beer can for him so that answered the question of what does he does in life.

He then said that he is friendly with everyone but does not like to get into a deep involvement as he did not want to put his thoughts into any ones mind as that would take away mental space from them.

Well interesting stuff to ponder on and its times like this that reminds me that if I chose to take the usual tourist route then I would miss this eccentric side of life.

Vision with the Elders

I met a third Elder Obelix at the Elders chill space who gives away free clothes and he made me giggle a bit as on our last fare well he took my hand and flirted with me which is why the name cos he was such a round and jolly fellow. There is a shortage of photos from Christiania by request from the natives as there are very private areas.

The last time I visited the Elders chill space I was tired so lay down on the low wall while Odin, Loki and Obelix were doing their usual thing of drinking canned beer smoking and talking and laughing.

I slept and upon awakening I was gifted with a last vision to take away to treasure and ponder over.

I awoke to find myself part of a full on vision in an ancient longboat with these three warriors Odin, Loki and Obelix and they all wore ancient battle gear with shields swords and winged helmets and the boat was floating very slowly toward a destination.

Odin had caught and held my eye as if he was aware of this vision and that he had invited me into this Warriors boat for a short time so I could bear witness to their last Sacred Journey.

Where after many years of doing battle, of not by wielding metal swords but the Spiritual Warriors sword of my generation that pioneered in our time the expansion of conciousness beyond generally accepted limitations.

They protected the conciousness of my generation that has love and spiritual awakening as its purpose and it felt like an honour had been bestowed upon me and I will never forget that moment and what I saw.

To my imagination it looked like they were being very slowly taken in the Viking Long Boat to Valhalla as honoured warriors by some very stoned Valkyry who were taking the scenic route and were not in a great hurry to arrive.

And again I am feeling such gratitude for these surreal experiences that fire my soul and inspire me to write magic stories.

Amsterdam Cannabis Socks

Later back in Midgard!

My diary said "Spent last night at hostel on a couch upstairs as a big drunk man lurched into my overspill cellar room with no windows and closed the door!"

Slightly scary stuff.

Home ward bound now across the cobbled pavements to the coach station cursing most of the way whilst dragging monster trolley and other and promising to never bring the big monster trolley out again and finding out that most coach drivers did not like the size of it.

Later when our German driver demanded five euros to take it on board I made an unexpected friend who gave me the fee which I gratefully accepted cos I had no cash on me and really I did not want to be stranded in Copenhagen.

Another short two hour ferry ride to Germany which was pleasant then another bus eventually waited at Berlin bus station for a few hours where I bought a souvenir penknife.

Another coach driver tried to charge me five euros extra for the monster four wheel trolley case but I was by now a hardened serial Monster Trolley Operator and so I faced him off with bold words and a special killer look and won.

Then on to another strange destination and a long wait outside a closed coach depot at 6 am in Beildfeld but eventually there was a very cool bus driver who did not give Trolley Monster a second look.

And I wondered if it had anything to do with the fact that the next destination was Amsterdam which is the land of laid back smoky folk.

Any way I enjoyed a pleasant bus journey and then we arrived at Amsterdam train station where I sat in a star bucks cos it had the only seat in the station and I charged the mobile then out on the pavement waiting for the bus to the UK I realised that I didn't have a souvenir from Amsterdam but fortunately there was a young man wearing socks with a cannabis leaf design so hey that was cool so I asked to take a photo of his socks and feet and I put it in my photo memory very quickly. And later Megi said she liked it and that made me very happy.

Oh just another near panic as flix bus double booked by 30 seats and so I just got on that bus cos the driver was English and I had a correct ticket code and he hated my monster trolley case but in a very English way did not make a fuss. My journey ended well even though the expected nice cup of English tea I was looking forward to on the ferry boat to UK was ghastly cos of strange milk.

Reflection

I didn't drink tea much but in Helsinki I craved it and was most grateful to receive a cup of strong Yorkshire tea from a fellow Brit at Outis.

And somehow my liking for the tea has revived now.

And to finally arrive home and deposit the monster trolley was such a huge relief as it had become a big secret stress point as all my paintings were in it and so the mission was to just get it home safe and I did promise to never ever take it on holiday again and I also agreed to Megan's suggestion that she supervise the packing next time.

Incidentally I count the whole paintings in the trolley event as one of the maddest things I have ever done.

The foraging season was a very long one due to a lack of rain and uncommonly warm weather so I kept going till the weather changed and this year I was introduced to the warmer climate of the Birch Tree Chaga in the form of a white fungus called Birch Poly Pore by my new friend Christine Fireheart and that held my attention for a long time.

I have discovered the absolute giving nature of this tree and I am full of respect for it now it's lifespan is the same as the human and even in its passing it just gives the most healing fruit. The Sami relied on it for its sap which is a healing drink the young leaves for tea, the bark for different things and I am sure used all of it for survival.

I had a pleasant surprise when I reconnected with Jerri on fb who did work at the fish stall at the market on the dock. He told me that he had given up working there and has now embraced his Sami culture and become a Shaman complete with a Sami Drum.

I recall that he made mention of his mother's Sami connection but he was always so busy working that we only ever had a few stolen moments of conversation that all that precious info never quiet sunk in to my mind.

I asked him for his story as and he began to speak of his Grandfather and Grandmother whom he clearly has a deep respect for who were both Sami I understood from his words that he has chosen to adapt his Shaman ways to modern life which I think is great cos he has a really friendly way about him and seems comfortable with his life.

I told him that he has now become part of the magic of my book and I really want to honour and support his Awakening by weaving his story in it. I am truly excited with anyone who can connect with their Ancestral origin as I have a deep connection with my own which began when my mother passed away. It began with my first concious focused inner journey. with my Mother where I learned to interpret their Other Worldly language of music visions and rhymes.

I have told him the story of my meeting with Eleena and he says that he may find her and that will be perfect.

Then Jerri fb message asking for clues what to take for a spiritual journey to Inari where he wants to connect with his ancestral spiritual roots.

I was really excited for him and was so glad to give him fb names of my three Pagan girl friends one of whom he has contacted already.

I also said briefly about the places of magic I had found including all the Sami places and so I will leave him there for now as this adventure of his is also his story that will probably take time to unfold and will be best told by him but I await this tale telling with big joy.

And the Sami are not so very far away to me as I recall that I have a friend Daniel who is a writer and great musician living in my village and he told me that he has a Sami grandmother.

This I did not know when I first met him but I found his energy so remarkably unusual then that I made mention of it to him at the time.

What energy did I see in him well the same as the first birch tree in Roveniemi that I made contact with and I do find that truly special.

I can't say why that was so I can only make a guess that the unity the Sami had with nature and the birch tree was so complete that it lives on in Ancestral cellular memory and in the energy field of the Sami even now.

It reminds me of a complete vision I had whilst on a sacred hill in England Solsbury Hill.

I was sitting near the top and then the veils of this world fell away revealing a very ancient North American village complete with authentic Tipis and then there was the presence of an Indian tribe and a hand from a warrior reached out into my world of now with love and wisdom and I felt a tremendous feeling of Wisdom and Love that was so powerful that it transcended time itself.

It was both an awesome and puzzling event but then when a few days later the Spiritual leader of the Shoshoni tribe visited the hill and performed a healing ceremony with ceremonial drum and a prayer for the desecrated land it made sense and I contemplated this event years later and feel that the power of the connection between the Native Indians and Mother Earth was such that it really did resonate and echoes still in the Realms of Mother Earth's energy fields even now thousands of years later. Not lost and not forgotten.

Someone said that the Sami ways are all lost and forgotten now but I beg to differ as my own personal experiences with my Ancestors show me that we carry all our ancestral memories in our cells both physically and spiritually and we just need to access them to remember and I know there will be someone who will effortlessly remember and become a beacon for others who want to remember with respect and reconnect with Nature.

I'm thinking perhaps Jerri could be that Shaman.

I'm not sure how old exactly the Sami culture is but my guess is it is probably at least as old as the North American Indian culture.

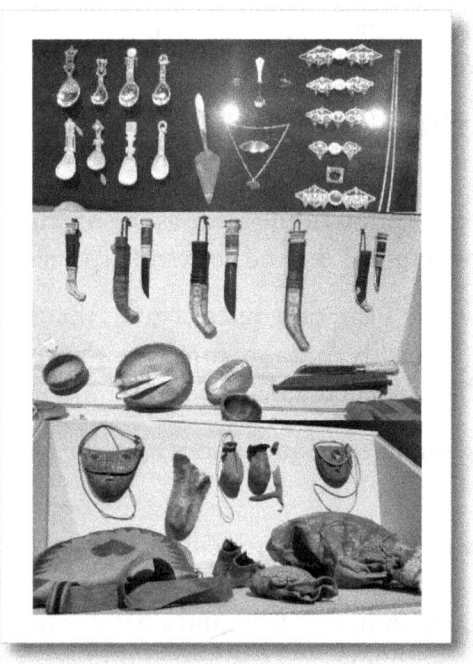

Understanding Metal music

I spent three years just breathing in the metal music experience and I have time to reflect now on my adventure and am ready to view some of the impressions I gained from the experiences.

When I have been at the two metal music festivals I have observed and listened to the fans and how they might experience metal music but I realise that not everyone can voice their opinion so they tend to say it just makes them feel good.

Metal music does not seem to hide from the shadow aspects of uncomfortable feelings but faces the dark part of humanity in total style.

Indeed loudly, theatrically, ceremoniously, poetically, profoundly, passionately, growlingly and shriekingly, melodically and as well as eloquently displaying the most vulnerable part of our human nature and our demons that we have learned to suppress because of modern societal pressures.

And in doing so it creates a bridge I feel from our inside most primal realms of the soul to the concious and complex world of now.

And other impressions I got that Metal music invites the listener to actually celebrate all emotions rather than avoid them which is accompanied by many expressive metal music styles and this to my mind is both inspirational and therapeutic of which you would not find in any therapy session that I know of.

I observed also that the whole mental structures of modern belief systems are totally challenged through metal music with songs revealing a shared experience of the souls longing for the ancient conciousness.

And I do share this longing myself as this ancient conciousness is not just about exorcising demons and shadows but about ancient shared soul Ancestral Memory that has both great meaning and beauty as it connects me the listener to ancient cultural roots and nurtures a true sense of belonging to nature a big tribe and indeed family which is really empowering. These are just early day thoughts.

Eluvietie's songs are all about the ancient Pagan ways of living and worship to the ancient Gods and reverence for nature and they have a huge fan base.

My band Wintersun eloquently and melodically challenge the whole structure of time itself and in this way I believe it did invite me to wake up to a more expanded spiritual reality in a very beautiful way.

And Jari Maenpaa has a unique ability to weave a depth of poetic passion and emotional expression throughout all his songs many of which are of nature and the seasons and having visited Finland it is easy for me to hear the atmosphere of the land through the music.

METAL MYSTICS TAKE ME

Starchild

Then there is this song Starchild that depicts perfectly the breaking down of mental structures and I will just show some lines from it here.

> Starchild.
>
> So mysterious is your world concealed beyond the stars Far away from the earth it flows one with time and dark as the night.
>
> Million shapes and colours are storming inside your mind Creating endless dimensions Forming Universes without walls.
>
> Let go of the stars that fell into the sea Let go of your thoughts and dreams what can you see now.
>
> You cannot save them any more Wanderer of time it is too late now Creator of Dimensions destroy the walls of time.
>
> Starchild Visions are born from the unknown force it dominates the Way of Time.
>
> The curtains of mist are fading and the veils of star clouds are revoked Storms of new energy flows in the depths of my mind.
>
> New Constellations are born in total harmony of perfection.
>
> And the dissonant unbalance was broken as the colours fall straight from the Light Starchild you fall like a burning star but there is no end to creation.

These are not the full words of the song all of which can be found on YouTube.

But for the first time listening I would recommend Time 1 as it is a total experience of musical styles and emotional tones.

Then there is the sound vibration and tones and pitch that give out from voice and electric guitar that I have experienced myself which acts as a carrier for healing energies that can both tonify the kidney energy and warm the heart and in a long cold winter that is pure medicine.

Indeed I have experienced a heavy metal band's music at Summerbreeze where I felt the sound vibration was acting like an aura cleanse on me.

And honestly It was and I am asking myself the burning question "Where does all this passion come from?"

For me it was like dimensional doors opened to reveal a Dragon Realm of eternal emotional expression inside a volcano that the singer was channelling and this for me was truly awesome.

And I recall that first audio exposure to Wintersun music opened the dimensional doors where visions were of an ancient time and Dragon energy and of course the vision of the White Goddess all delivered through the music where it transformed into energy colour and wave length and great feeling.

And I have realised that one thing about metal music that keeps me hanging on is simply the musical expression of passion the kind I believe that was once my own natural expression of the joy for life itself probably eons ago.

Here is the another thing now I remember that my love of metal music coincided with the waking up of my inner warriors so I guess it is my warrior music, though not a sword carrying more the spiritual warrior kind.

Where the passion fuelled my sacred journey which also inspired a vision of the ancient Goddess and Warriors that took me to Finland and inspired me to connect with my band and had me travelling and living on a trust that took me right out of my comfort zone onto the edge.

But then it seemed that out of a situation of near disaster some thing surprising and truly magic always happened like seeing the Northern Lights creating a new art form for myself and discovering the story telling stones.

Then finding my inner story teller and meeting my guitar hero Teemu Mäntysaari on the metro.

And seriously as Morgana said what are the chances of that happening? and then having an unforgettable guitar lesson with him. Magic.

Meeting strange people and drinking pure sweet water in Finland and all the visions. Indeed I would feel that this my Spiritual journey did place me in a State of Grace where by I was guided to go where I needed to be placed in the Magic Zone without too much discomfort.

I think about my generation that had the love but we were young in time and did not know how to deal with shadow self and we had forgotten our own ancient Pagan soul connection and culture so we looked to another ancient culture to define our connection to spirit which brought Guru worship and meditation.

So that was an interesting time and although I did not ever close up from the conciousness of it I just found my inner warrior and recalibrated my own spiritual compass.

As this metal music holds a deep ancient spiritual warrior connection for me which was triggered when I first heard Wintersun the best way I can describe it is with a poem I wrote that began as a vision inspired by their music and an ancient sacred landscape It remained mostly as that until recently when all the words just arrived.

Metal Mystics

Wizards and Warriors awoke
Down the Passage of Time
To a Darker Sun and Brighter Stars
Forsaking Wands Swords and Spells that Rhyme
for the Magic of Drums and Electric Guitars

Incantations now Sung
To Melodic Notes played
Does Fire my Soul and Enchant my Eyes
As it bids me recall Sacred Warrior Oaths made
Under Ancient Green and Magenta Skies

I knew that metal music had a passionate nature and lived in its own realm far beyond the confines of the third dimension as it had the power to create sound that could vibrate producing goose bumps on a cellular level and visions in the soul and my experience is that all this sound could be effortlessly channelled through electric guitar and voice.

There were all the aspects of metal music experience floating around in my mind along with a growing need to bring them all together and put an actual name to this metal music phenomenon.

And so I intensified my inner search for a reason Why I experienced such a full on explosion of energy the first time of hearing Metal Music because it was certainly not a normal event and I needed to honour and celebrate it as one would in any situation of experiencing such a powerful cosmic event.

What and Why Metal Magic

I was asking WHAT is the Magic and WHY is the Magic and this question became like a mantra that I silently repeated for days on end.

Till one day my persistence was rewarded in a one word to describe all this phenomena as it revealed itself as a FREQUENCY.

And then it all made sense to me and for some time I was calling it The Frequency of Passion.

And I realised that is what I had been following since I first heard the music.

Indeed I believe that the impact when first I heard it was so very powerful because it carried that real Frequency which stayed for the whole of the car journey and even now when travelling on a comfortable bus I turn on I tunes put on ear plugs and listen to Time I.

And there are pockets of sound from both Jari Mäenpää's voice and electric guitar and harmonies from the band that creates the perfect pitch to put shivers in my head a longing in my heart and tears in my eyes. And actually a dance in my soul which some day my earthly feet might just learn to trace the steps to in this world. and I wonder if this is all that its about why folk just love all this metal sound to get Taken by the FREQUENCY.

Another unexpected bit of magic occurred recently concerning the metal music when my friend Sam who does laughter therapy was sitting in my living room and I had just told her about my love for metal music "Its a frequency" she said which both delighted and shocked me a little as I had not long discovered that thought myself and believed it just lived in my mind.

She then said with utter confidence that the musical sound was not new and had been heard in ancient times. Well I had to believe it was possible given my experience with it.

Then later on a warm summers day whilst sitting in the green countryside garden of Meg and her boy friend Joe I began to converse with him about the metal music and as he is a trained musician he has many different examples of music on CDs one of which is of an ancient Mongolian chant which is sung in a very deep voice from the belly.

Joe said it could be similar to the sound emanating from various metal music singing techniques and I am remembering that the Buddhist chant of Aum, that is considered to be a very spiritual, has been scientifically proven to be the actual sound that the Sun makes.

Clever Buddhists Huh? Powerful stuff.

All the times ever I have sat with Krishna folk when they are chanting I have experienced easily the essence of their spirituality and can well believe that they are tuning in to a very high spiritual frequency which gets them really high.

I was becoming now really interested to know of the origins of this metal music so I searched on line found out that it actually began in the late sixties. Bands like Black Sabbath, Judas Priest and Led Zeppelin seeded heavy metal music from late sixties /early seventies and then I read that the biggest metal influence was from the band Iron Maiden who are still making albums. Hmm I wonder how they all feel about creating this music and knowing that it has evolved and flowered from its origins of heavy metal to all kinds of musical expressions.

I think they should feel justifiably proud.

Who would have ever thought back in the heavy metal days that there would be such sweet and harmoniously melancholic expressions that would pour out of this strange metallic flower and that in its unfolding it would open ancestral portals and access universal frequencies and create a vehicle of such great passion and meaning which could not only heal but unite so many people in friendship and love.

And who could not say that metal does not have the power to heal and I would love to see a t shirt with words printed on it. METAL HEALS.

Miguels Magic Metal Story

And I feel that this story will not easily end in the writing of it as most recently again I met by chance another metal fan whom I met at the Crop Circle symposium in Glastonbury his name is Miguel and he is a serious writer.

I felt instinctively to ask him if he liked metal music and after the big Yes he did he treated me to the story of his first contact with metal music.

This unexpected meeting greatly inspired me and led me to decide to ask other metal fans about their first experience with metal music and as I was going to the Summerbreeze metal festival because my band Wintersun were playing there for the first time since 2014 and it felt right that I took my questions there.

Wolf and Vera

On the 11th of august I got a coach to Frankfurt where my metal friends Wolf and Vera from the previous Summerbreeze festival had offered to collect me as a guest at their house before and after the festival.

Wolf arrived in a big car and we travelled with the roof down as it was a really warm day and I heard for the first time the melodic fantasy band Epica which has a female singer with a beautiful clear voice and I was for the first time Taken to the frequency of it Beautiful.

When we arrived I was made very comfortable in my own guest room and the next day Vera created a huge amazing barbecue for us and the extra expected friends there was Natalie with her partner Micheal with Martin and Obi with Alex.

Collecting Metal Stories

I took this opportunity to ask the three young folk about their first metal music experience and I was really moved by their stories. (I have put them all together in order with other later festival stories for the sake of easy reading in the book) We all travelled to Dinkelsbühl the next day in extreme weather of very hot followed by stormy downpours all the way but Wolf and Vera's camper van protected us and offered much comfort.

Tarde Journeyman

Then we gave a lift to a young man named Tarder to Summerbreeze who was wearing what looked like a national costume and his story is this.

He had just completed his apprenticeship as a boat builder and was following the medieval tradition of travelling away from his home for three years to find work with other companies and in that time he is not allowed to go back to within 50 kilometres of his own home and must rely on the good nature of people to house him for the nights.

I think these boys are called Journey Men and I did so admire him.

We took him to the main entrance where he planned to ask for work in return for enjoying the festival and after eighteen months of being out there I felt he deserved a break.

SUMMERBREEZE 2017

We camped in the Green camping area when we arrived at Summerbreeze festival site which was supposed to be quiet and clean I took Vera's advice and paid 12 euros extra for the use of all the warm showers I wanted and flush toilets. The festival I am most used to is Glastonbury where generations of us used the low tech toilet which was a huge deep dug out ditch with sort of wooden plank seats resting across the pit and the user would mostly hold the nose and not look down!

That was the Green Way!

Summerbreeze festival site is an enormous amount of farmland where there still was surrounding fields of very big corn on the cob growing with the main separated festival site with cut grass.

I had a pop up tent and an air bed and Wolf sorted both these tricky things for me then after all caravans with awnings etc was all sorted it absolutely poured down a full on lightning storm and I did not sleep well so I had my first sleep deprivation experience there since 2014.

YAAY DINKELSBÜHL

The following day it was sunny again and I walked bare foot to the shower place which was great and then did gratefully take the free shuttle bus to Dinkelsbühl and it was a deeply emotional experience for me as I recalled my first time there with Megan and Morgana helping me and I bathed in the absolute charm and beauty of this place as it is a really exceptional town with every house built in antiquity.

I had noticed the architecture more this time which revealed a city wall that I believe once totally enclosed the town and it still is adorned with turrets and old stone houses built into it then it reaches the faery tale castle with big round towers and on one of the tower windows is a huge long yellow plait just hanging down.

I imagine it has to do with the faery tale of Rapunzel and I was charmed by it and with the castle being surrounded by a big lake that just perfectly completes the absolute magical atmosphere of this remarkable place.

I bought food stuff at the local supermarket and took a few photos of long haired metal fans buying provisions.

METAL MYSTICS TAKE ME

Meeting Vlad who was Bnaap

I had just crossed the road when a van honked loudly at me and a very big hand attached to a very big arm waved enthusiastically at me out the open window which I discovered after focusing on the spectacle all belonged to my metal friend BNAAP!!! SINCRINISTIC OR WOT.

Well that was a surprise so we connected and I bought him good German beer from the supermarket not quiet as cool as the beer making restaurant but he was needing to sign in at Summerbreeze so we planned to meet later. (Just a short note here to say that the security was so much nicer this year)

Finding Luca and Virna

I was on the way to see my first band the following day when I found Virna's partner Luca so we all had a great happy reunion and watched Power Wolf band together after I told them of my meeting with Bnaap they showed that they call him Vlad well that made sense so I will call him Vlad who was Bnaap.

This festival was a total sensory experience again for me but this time I had listened to Vera's choice in metal bands at her home and in her car and when I heard something I liked a lot I then enquired who it was and in this way I was able to build up a modest selection of bands to see at Summerbreeze. (Virna gifted me with a 2016 beaker that has all the band names.) Grazi Bella.

I came across a small area that was home to some life size wooden stage props all donated by the group like an ancient longboat and for statues.

So Vlad and I posed for some pictures among this thing cos strangely there was a photo camera but we did the mobile pics as well and the result I thought were pretty good.

My food bringing to Germany in 2014 had not been forgotten and was still out there as a good joke so when I related to Wolf that one of the scare tactics to keep UK in the EU was a warning of food scarcity he then said with great humour that he would bring me food to England from Germany in that eventuality. Wow what a friend haha.

My band Wintersun were playing at the main stage on friday but on Thursday. I visited Dinkelsbühl again and sat with Vlad who was Bnaap outside our favourite restaurant that makes its own beer and I actually ordered a soup that was really great and decided that buying camping food whilst in a piddly tent with a teeny tiny solid fuel stove to cook on was really boring and eating out had defiantly more flavour.

Swimming in the River

After listening in fascination to Vlad's first metal music experience and writing it down I walked to the river there were a few young metal fans and after securing an agreement to catch their metal stories.

I dived in for a short swim which was utterly divine as the river was warm and softly flowing then after I asked the lovely boy Roman the story of his first metal experience and the answer he gave touched my heart deeply.

Then whilst waiting for the shuttle bus I saw an older woman standing amongst all the metal fans who were also waiting and I talked with her as I didn't know if she felt nervous to be there but turns out she was more than fine.

"They never fight" she said and gladly consented to be photographed with one very colourful metal fan and then when her son arrived they both agreed for me to take a picture of them both. (Renate and Felix, danke schön)

The following day it was still very hot and I regretted not swimming in the river again as an extreme weather warning at the festival warned of a big storm and it came with a plea for everyone to take care of each other.

The warning was true in part at least as heavy rain occurred at sixish whilst just having seen Epica on main stage which was lovely and the keyboard player had a half rounded key board that he crowd surfed a little with.

The band sounded like melodic fantasy metal to me.

The sky turned dark and none of us knew if we would see any more of our bands playing such was the gravity of the situation.

Then it poured down and I rushed back to base camp in a very wet best green lace dress and changed into leather jeans and our green gate security man Lou who I had daily pleasant chats with whilst coming and going to the green camping field I thought he was really cool and friendly and that day he gave me his emp rain wear complete with hood so I was sorted against all weather odds. (Thanks dude)

Wintersun cancelled their autograph signing I think due to fatigue but showed up later to play before then however I had a four hour wait in the elements listening to bands I did not chose.

Miguel had gifted me with a pink scarf from Glastonbury and I told him that I would have a picture taken of it crowd surfing but alas I was so confused about the audience location that it did not happen.

WINTERSUN at MIDNIGHT GIG

As I saw just a few folk near the stage and with a strange barrier system keeping me from getting there I then did assume that it was for VIPs only and I could not gain entrance to be close to my band and so endured being outside and a fair distance away with also many more Wintersun fans who must have thought the same thing.

It was the next day when we heard that they had just changed how one could get to the front of the stage AARGH TWICE NOW I am denied the happy ever after moment of being physically close to my favourite band as they play live.

Wintersun are always great on stage live but I could not see them clearly as so many stage lights and although I could hear them my iPhone did not pick up a clean sound or clear video picture so I had to just let it all go. (Or suffer a lot)

My festival t shirt had a blue wolf logo which I liked but I dropped and lost it the next day. Well I just hoped that someone deserving found it and was thrilled. I had discovered that there were plastic beakers with the festival logo printed on and a lovely young man Christian kindly sold me six of them six being 2017 and one from 2014 so there we were with souvenirs.

Crowdsurfing Love in

The next day was sunny and I saw a great melodic death metal band called Dark Tranquillity which was not previously on my radar and the special thing about it was the lead singer Mikael Stanne.

With his angelic golden curly hair went to the audience and touched and shook hands and lovingly hugged and kissed a man in a wheelchair and then everyone else whilst singing and then cos it was a 20th birthday of the Summerbreeze Metal festival he asked everyone if they would crowd surf him to the emp tower across the way which was a long way at least 100 yards I'd guess.

This spectacle was already beginning to melt my heart and when he climbed the protection fence and shimmied over then melted into the obviously loving arms of adoring fans. WOW.

It began to work on a very deep emotional level with me as I was being reminded of the very first time I saw this crowd surfing event that drew tears from me and at that time I was not fully concious of all the reasons why and I was being distracted with filming but this experience would later allow form to the many emotions and give them names.

He now looked totally at home and made a handsome show with his black clothes and his golden hair with legs in deep relax mode and set apart so that the fans could hold pretty much most of his body with his head sometimes tilted back in absolute surrender trusting strangers albeit loving with his safety whilst still holding a mic and singing.

And apart from the keyboard player from Epica having a quick surf this was the first time I had seen a metal band singer crowd surf before.

Watching this now became most evocative for me now as I have not seen so many hands crowd surfing a body like this before and all the hands holding him gave the impression to me of being tiny petals of a huge flower gently moving in the breeze as they were bearing this captured treasure over a vast ocean of bigger waves and though the weather was not great he really did make the sun shine in my heart. ABSOLUTE THERAPY.

And when he had reached the emp tower and wished them all a happy 20th birthday and then asked to be surfed back.

I took a few pics of that event and left with a lighter spirit in me.

Crowdsurfing What a great gift Firstly to experience it in the beginning and then this time to experience a whole new aspect which evoked so much so I will begin with saying.

I find It is like a secret unspoken language Why No one says "Hey will you lift me up?"

I'm going up to totally let my body go limp to be carried by so many strangers and while this is happening I will be in an ecstatic state of complete surrender that everyone surfing me understands.

Crowdsurfing hopefuls just usually lift up their arms as a child might do for a carry or hug (and I believe that you need to have the trust of a child to place your safety in the hands of strangers) but there are always fans to lift you up and carefully pass you from one group of hands to another.

And this I believe is a real family tribe bonding effort as it demands skill and a consistent caring and believe me when so many hands are holding you and carefully moving you along at arms length.

It is like having a wibbely wobbly hug and from what I felt Going Up that it felt natural and I did feel safe and accepted as part of the big event.

Some reflection as time passed brought the belief that I was so moved by my first sight of crowd surfing because it was the element of absolute trust shown that I had lost as I grew up replacing it with armour and shields.

And for me to embrace being crowd surfed myself was a healing for that inner child. The band Power Wolf have a T Shirt with the words Metal is a Religion printed across the front of it and I am thinking that if that is the case then the festival site is the Church and the stage is the Alter and the band are the Shaman or Mystics.

The devotee or fan could show their devotion in this way to be carried to the nearest point where the band was and if Metal is a religion then I see crowd surfing as a Sacrament/Blessing.

When Dark Tranquillity singer Mikael Stanne placed himself completely in the hands of the fans it looked like a magic alchemical fusion of pure love and trust and it was the nearest thing to a LOVE IN I have witnessed since the hippie days of the sixties.

And yes "It is all Too Beautiful" And it is All That.

You could not buy this experience and it was a beautiful end to a deeply meaningful festival. And it made me want to return for Summerbreeze and the metal family the music and swimming in the river in Dinkelsbühl again.

I saw Tarder on the last day at the festival so I knew he d been accepted to work and he then told me that he had been offered a job mending boats on a small Italian island where they rescue boat refugees and I enjoyed seeing him again and most heartily wished him very well.

I had found my festival legs by day three and felt really great from walking in the open air all the five days.

Time to leave then and a bit sad about it as I was just getting into it.

So then we packed up and left for home with just one hiccough when the camper broke down owing to a tiny metal piece that releases the gas.

After calling the breakdown system it looked like we d be there for four hours cos lots of vehicles needed a start up after running the battery down from listening to Metal Music at the festival.

I just looked around the grass verges and found at least twelve different kinds of wild flowers and then a hazel nut tree with really big hazels.

Then after only thirty mins the mechanic showed up and fixed everything so we returned to Wolf and Vera's home where Vera continued to take such good care of me.

Pizza Ice Cream and the Rhine

My blue jeans were really muddy and I gratefully accepted a black pair from her.

A trip to the city Mainz with a special natural ice cream treat by the Rhine river which is flanked by big beautiful green trees where Wolf said as a young man he and some friends swam across and ended up 20 kilometres down river as the currant was so strong.

Then on to the old town and a pizza place from his youth yum yum.

As we walked along the Rhine there were very unusual trees that the bark on the trunks reminded me of an impressionist painting as they had small pieces of bark that fell away easily showing a smooth trunk of light yellow green that gave the impression of it emanating its own light.

Wolf offered some deep thoughts as he said the trees were older than the second world war and he pondered on what sights they had born witness to.

Eventually it was time to leave.

Wolf and Vera drove me to the bus station in Frankfurt which I was most grateful for late in the evening as my coach was midnight time.

Farewell Wolf and Vera

Fond farewells followed by quiet a good nights sleep was welcomed and when we reached the ferry French side the passport control took it very well when I protested my bag being scanned and they just looked inside.

The epi pen and antihistamine I showed them was totally a mystery and I had to explain three times their use but we were sailing more when I showed the left over onions and garlic and by the time I presented the large piece of raw ginger a state of understanding was reached and they were all totally cool with my stuff.

I recall my daughter in law JuJu asking me after a great meal she cooked for us "WHY DID YOU TAKE GINGER TO HELSINKI" "Because its organic" I answered confidently but now I will have fun telling her how it bridged the great language divide of English traveller and French border control.

Just show onions first then garlic and lastly the ginger and walk away hassle free.

The First Metal Music Experiences

The sky in England sadly was that surreal grey all the way home but I stayed home a while to sort my bomb site of a flat out then glorious Brighton beach and swimming for a few days.

Festivals are all about INCOMING!! with constant sound and sites and weather so only after do I sit and reflect on my thoughts of this festival time which were about unexpected meetings with special folk who by opening their hearts to me and sharing their stories of their first metal music experiences opened my eyes and heart and I feel so much richer for that in understanding and so it is with gratitude that I offer these precious tales.

These are the stories from people about their first metal music experience the first I offer is from my friend Miguel told at the Glastonbury crop circle symposium.

Miguel's Magic Metal Music Memory

He was sitting with new friends I believe and the first time he heard metal music felt like an explosion in his head with the energy surging through all the cells of his being and the journey this new music took him on ended with him having a very big environmental job globally. (yes really)

Miguel is a very eloquent speaker so it was a joy to listen to his first metal experience as he described the event in terms of dynamic energies in a most animated way using his hands to describe it, which created a beautiful out pouring of energy for me to see and I could relate to it and after ward I was so inspired that it seeded the idea to ask others about their first metal music experience.

Natalie's story told in Wolf and Vera's garden

Her father was into metal and at age two was the first special time when she actually felt the Vibration of the music.

At 16 whilst listening to a Man of War song she felt Tingles "Like Electricity" she said and then she just Tuned in to the Energy of Mother Nature. Where she then became aware of the environment and the damage we do to it. At age 28 Natalie can still Tune in to Mother Nature when she hears metal music.

Natalie's story was unexpected and the part about tuning in to Mother Nature just brought tears to my eyes.

Later I contemplated why and its because she also had found the most surprising and unlikely connection from Metal Music to Divine Earth Energy which was also most similar to my experience when I saw the White Goddess and this felt like a treasure to me now.

Micheal's story told in Wolf and Vera's garden.

At 16 ish he heard the song Moondance from the band Nightwish which is melodic death metal and for the first time he actually felt the music and it opened his heart and still does. He now likes Hammerfall and melodic Goth.

Micheal is a sensitive looking man who appeared to be not very open but as soon as he consented to give me his story his energy seemed right from the heart and I felt privileged that he would show that to me.

Wolf's story from his garden.

At 14 he saw a picture of a metal musician with long hair who became his hero and after he connected with the music and he still has the album.

The name of the band was Led Zeppelin.

He says that Beethoven and Bach were considered the punks of their day and ridiculed like metal music is today but the classics are immortalised now in western culture.

Wolf likes to hear singing voices used like instruments.

and when we were driving in his car with Epica playing I experienced the energy of her voice through Wolf's eyes as it were and I have to say that it was a lovely energy.

Vera's story from her home.

Vera is also my friend and I did not press her for details about her statement cos one the language barrier and two I understood she was referring to endorphins that are triggered in her from metal music.

Vera says that when she plays heavy metal at home then she feels that all is right and good in her world.

Martin's Story told in Wolf and Vera's garden.

At 13ish he saw Rammstein at a concert with an impressive fire show which enriched his experience of the music and Amon Armoth is his favourite band and opens his heart and when they play guitar riffs it sets off a tingle effect and he says that some metal music calms him down.

Martin has a kindly character and easy going too and it was great to hear about the tingle effect again.

Alex's Story told in Wolf and Vera's garden.

At 13ish heard Linkin Park which felt exciting and he says that it is also calming and he said this "When they scream then I don't have to" his Mother was worried that listening to metal music would make him aggressive but is cool with that now Alex's words were simple but really profound and reminded me of the Shamanistic aspect of metal bands exorcising negative energies (simple genius)

Andreas' story told at Summerbreeze festival.

At 13ish Waken festival in the Mosh Pit where he felt explosions of overwhelming energy that he did not know before and enabled him to let loose and go crazy where he really felt emotionally a part of everyone dancing with him like it was his family all sharing the same experience.

Andreas was 13ish which is the natural age to experience the Rites of Passage and if the dance experience was that then I feel it was so beautifully done that I wish I had been there and I think Meg would not have been too worried and it answers a question for me about shared metal experience. (And he did say Dancing)

Sarah Lee's Story told at Summerbreeze festival.

Came from a classical music back ground to Rammstein and "It was like entering a new universe through a black hole" and "Hearing Wintersun was like heavens gate opening" she said.

This is the teenager I met when we were all waiting for Summerbreeze to arrive at a Meet and Greet signing of autographs and then they cancelled and she was very upset and her grief touched me and her story was she had drawn a picture of Jari Mäenpää and was really wanted to give it direct to him and then no one in security would or could take it to him. In an attempt to cheer her up I told her of the guitar lesson I had with Teemu Mäntysaari and the generosity of him showing me the Sonic Pump recording studio and I showed her the pics still on my iPhone then I asked her story. The way she described the whole experience evokes visions in me of invisible dimensional doors opening and I wonder if one day she will say those words herself.

Roman's Story told on the river steps in Dinkelsbühl

He identifies with being a scientist and a geek who listened to video games music but not connecting emotionally with it then he heard the metal band Extremo and for the first time felt the overwhelming emotions and very deep messages.

Roman said "My scientific self will look at a beautiful river and only see it as H_2O and will view the world in the same emotionally disconnected way and its this part of me that suffers from depression"

When he listens to metal music it connects him to his real feelings and his soul

So he then can connect with the rest of humanity.

This he said are the two personalities existing in him.

He said "Metal is the other of me that is different that gets to me and gives me hope" Roman says that Extremo are all about freedom and passion.

This meeting felt so special as I believed I was hearing a deep soul retrieval experience. This gentle young man with a sensitive face melted my heart that day and I am so grateful to have his story in the book.

The Tao of Vlad

Vlad who was Bnaap's Story told outside a restaurant in Dinkelsbühl.

As a young man in Ukraine he first heard Nirvana on a player that he d rested on the back of his head and he says.

His aggression goes down like a wall of fire then he closes his eyes and listens he said "It's like dropping into a deep big space without borders which is different to mind or mental space as this one has no dimensions also like dropping into a big ocean and swimming."

"The memories of my metal music exist in the many places in my mind" he said Vlad made it his mission in his city to record and make available great music for everyone who wanted to hear it also.

I was aware that Vlad's answer would be quiet at home in a Zen Monastry being quoted by an old Master. Totally mind blowing and really silenced me and so unexpected from a big swarthy looking Ukraine type with very long thick brown hair and if you didn't get acquainted with this part of his nature you could miss the deep nature of this being which I was in danger of doing beforehand.

Patrick's Story told by the river steps in Dinkelsbühl

He came from a punk music tradition and was bullied at school for having long hair.

Metal music had lots of energy for him and helped him overcome hard times.

Patrick was very friendly and I was glad to hear that metal helped him deal with bullying.

Virna's Story sent electronically (she is my friend)

At 6ish she heard Alice Cooper and Poison which she listened to a lot.

At 12 she read The Flowers of Evil by Charles Baudelaire and she related to the poem like the poem could read her empty heart.

Not many friends at school cos she didn't fit in the mould of skinny girl and she loved books so she was ridiculed by boys.

She found Nirvana and Guns and Roses.

She says "Metal music has rage in them and also a light that makes me feel fine again."

Their poetry put some feeling in her heart.

Her dad bought her the Metalica Lyrics in 1992 she says "When I read text Nothing else matters I understood that metal would be the way I would live and the text So close no matter how far is from the heart Forever trusting who we are and nothing else matters.

I think metal is the way to survive as there must be rage or melancholy and sadness in everyday of our lives but we have to smile.

We are Warriors and we always live to win and as a lot of metal music says.

Our hearts are of steel and we'll always look to the future knowing that we'll never walk alone." (Grazia Bella Virna)

I did not want to change any of Virna's words as she is Italian and I was really glad to hear her story cos I felt that for the first time I was understanding her true Nature Deep respect Bella and glad you're my friend.

I thought this was all the stories but then I realised that I had left someone really important out of the metal stories so I called Scott.

Scott's Story on the phone to my home.

His thoughts went like this.

"Metal is a way of looking at yourself and it has a strong energy to it that amps every thing up giving it a structure.

like joining a currant that has purpose in life a direction that is very enjoyable" when there were musical clips on the manga and anime video like The Heart Beneath by Celtic Cross he got swept up travelling into a mindscape and "The guitar riff it really tugs at you" he said.

Scott says it gives energy and fills you with hope and positivity evoking fantasy and grand landscapes painting art in your mind which is really good.

Scott liked the band Opeth a lot but will listen to many other bands now also.

He says that metal is much more evocative than other music as it has so many component parts and it does connect him to his feelings.

He will pick a genre depending on what mood he is in he says cos it helps him get back in touch with something he couldn't before "It's like opening a little valve" he said.

* * *

I was in Scott's car when I first heard his CD of Wintersun and he was the friend who kindly turned up the volume very high and I remembered four years ago in his car and he showing me the tingle effect on his arm where the hairs were standing up. Bless you babe I am understanding you better now and you have been in my life for four years so I am wondering now "Blimey What else have I missed?"

So I have arrived full circle on an adventure that has both challenged and changed my life ……

But the story is not over cos the whole experience continues to create beauty and transformation in my world and there are some loose ends also as I did not get to talk to Teemu Mäntysaari about the frequency of metal music and I would really love that opportunity in the future to do that.

Then the other subject of being a good guitar pupil as I promised.

Well I am still cutting my nails short for playing electric guitar but it took so long for me to get an electric guitar which my son eventually bought me that I lost the thread of learning what I had and I had problems with noise level where I live and I got so stressed with all that but this Journal kept calling me to write it and eventually I had to pay heed to it.

So many humble apologies Master Mäntysaari but I will get back to it as soon as this book project is safely tucked up in bed.

Every time I go away I seem to have gained a new and unexpected treasure and when I think about this last and fourth journey away to a Metal Festival the thing that I have come away with are the friendships forged with Wolf and Vera and all the support they gave me with sharing their home and keeping me safe and being able to laugh with them and eat pizza and ice cream and Vera is such a great cook and has a great nurturing nature that I felt really safe and comfortable.

Then there's the special stories from folk who opened up to me and gave me such a deeper understanding of themselves through their relationship to metal music.

Some questions also answered about the Metal family idea and I certainly was made to feel like part of that and of course it adds fathomless depths to the Metal experience in the book and I am sure has greatly enhanced my understanding of Metal Heads. Precious.

My inner reflections on the music are about frequency and vibration but recently I have been focusing on the words of the songs of the bands that I like and the message they convey as that is where I find a religious/pagan influence.

The subject of the immortality of the soul was key in Paganism then when it fell prey to other religious dogma the reality of communicating directly to the Divine was suppressed along with another subject about Ancestral connection.

For example when I first connected consciously with my ancestors some years past I became aware that this was a Divine Birthright and then what followed was the realisation that this ancient right was also suppressed and has been forgotten now by most folk.

But some truths are so obvious to me and cannot be buried for ever and when I began to listen to the metal music words I saw unfolding a musical revolution that was actually displaying a great DEPROGRAMING PROCESS of all the misinformation and cultural conditioning and who can say that its not raising conciousness quiet like a dynamic meditation would do. (Albeit rather loud)

(Big WOW moment that was)

And it seems to me like the band members are the Metal Mystics performing a Sacred Ritual with music in order to burst through and exorcise all of that misinformation.

A sort of Chucking it Back.

And I am thinking that it takes a real courage to tell the truth and then to constantly hold on and embody it and this is how I see the metal musicians as Warriors on the front line in the battle for truth and freedom.

Which is another element that I experience when I hear the words of the songs and I really admire that and I think that it triggers my own inner warrior courage. And yes of course I am aware that truth can be found in many other ways but Metal Music played by Metal Mystics was my choice because I feel there are many aspects to metal because that same level of musical pitch and tone makes magic happen and opens portals, and accesses frequencies.

And that does I am delighted to say appear to be the Way of Metal Music.

I am thinking about the vision of an ancient sky and Northern Lights and a Goddess with ancient warriors all inspired by the music of my Wintersun band which is where my poem began about Metal Mystics and in that very long ago place I certainly would have worshipped the goddess of Nature.

But I was still trying to weave her harmoniously into the big story with metal music when a friend visited.

Kat as I discovered has a rare talent of listening from a deep Pagan place and as I shared my logistical reflections she was right there with the absolute right words to bring a perspective both about Goddess energy and metal music.

Of metal music she said this "The bad reputation that metal has (certainly in the UK) is like a shield to protect it from being co opted to mainstream music where they would take the wild and rebellious spirit out of it." Hmmm.

Of the Shaman aspect she spoke of the three levels in Celtic religion at the bottom is the underworld of ancestors where shadows would be called up into the middle magic elemental realms and the top is the higher world where the energy is transformed.

And it becomes clearer for me to see this Shamanic process occurring in metal music so I wonder "Are we all taking this Sacred Journey?"

About the frequency she said "Its like connecting with and tuning in to a global SAT NAV" And I did so like that thought. (Blessed Be Kat) clever words.

The Goddess is from ancient times before history when all of Nature was regarded as a Sacred Temple and we all knew Mother Natures Names as I am sure that all creatures see Mother Nature in their own image she was seen as the Divine aspect of Mother Earth made manifest in our human eyes as a beautiful Mystical Woman.

Kat said something about finding the Formless Form of the Goddess.

(Quiet Zen) and for me it was like seeing her as the Yin element to the Yang force of metal as in this way they are apparently opposites but with an intimate divine connection that intertwines as it weaves music and vision together and I recall Natalie's metal experience of tuning in to Mother Earth and I think for me now it is a Divine Mystery not to be over analysed but instead cherished as a sacred gift.

So that is what I am doing remembering also the painted puzzle with the missing piece now more intently as this adventure with all the different aspects deepens I have begun to view it as pieces of a puzzle that are being drawn together to make one complete picture in my life.

Honouring the Ancestors

Before this adventure began I was first reading about frequencies which appeared to belong to a magic landscape and this was a new word that I felt unable to grasp the meaning of.

I felt that I really needed to know so that I may connect with the true Nature of

Mother Earth and my own spiritual evolution but being unable to grasp and remember logical information I felt shut out of a crucial part of me.

But as I am guided by my Ancestors and knowing they seldom communicate with me in a straight line as it were but more with visions music poetry and energy and so it would seem that in this way with every piece of this puzzle fitting into place they are featuring as a support on my journey and helping me learn about frequencies through metal music.

Well and why not Metal music.

It has passion just like Italian opera and the more I listen to metal the more I get the feeling it has more in common with opera than not.

Indeed lots of different metal styles have this operatic expression and it is usual to get a mix between the growl y voice with thrash and operatic tones.

I am also being reminded now that previous to this journey I would only communicate with my matriarchal ancestors which was a bit unbalanced (although it did create a strong and respectful foundation for connecting with the divine feminine) And so now I understand that part of the puzzle pieces are connected with the healing of the patriarchal aspect of my inner ancestors.

(Nicely done with metal music) I am thinking with a smile on my face gratitude in my heart and a few tears in my eyes.

"But Why the Tears There" "It's All Too Beautiful."

(Now I really didn't think that I was gonna write that again) Since I first became aware of them in my life and with all the insight and guidance they have given me I am steadily come to believe that so much that I do in my life now is a training for me to take my place among them (eventually) also and become a good Ancestor myself.

METAL MYSTICS TAKE ME

The Big Birthday

But meanwhile back on Mother Earth It was soon to be what I refereed to as my Big Birthday and traditionally I didn't make a fuss and so the birthdays with a few exceptions (fish n chips with Meg) crept by almost unseen and previously my vanity insisted on keeping my age a secret but just a few weeks before this one a change occurred where it became really important to me that This One be acknowledged by all of my family as a celebration cos it did begin to feel that way to me.

I really wanted to share this new found positive attitude with my twin so I wrote on the birthday card I sent her "The next 70 years will be a lot easier" Then around my family I let it be known that I did want a fuss made this year and I was calling it My Big Birthday.

My son Marcus called and said "A big birthday! Probably with a zero."

Yes of course with a zero and I told Mathew that 70 is cool and I was looking forward to the next 70 years cos I am just only NOW getting the hang of being ME..

My daughter in law JuJu and son Mathew's home was to be the celebration venue and I arrived to an astonishing display of birthday spirit in the form of a huge long decorated table with silver balloons and a big YAY silver balloon thing hanging on the ancient oak structured wall of the room that made me laugh.

The tantalising food sights and aromas from the kitchen completed the feast of the senses all created by Ju Ju Goddess in the kitchen.

Mathew led me to the birthday table with the words "Here is your Fuss" (That boy of mine just has a way with words) It was a full on amazing day and I gave out the printed Summerbreeze 2017 beakers to my family that I wrapped in the pages of a German metal music magazine.

The beakers I gave had some sentimental value and some amusement when my daughter read out some of the stranger Metal Band names printed on it I was invited to say something wise but all previous ideas of what to say vanished so I began to tell a story about crowd surfing (rather badly) and then there was a hush followed soon after by relief and a few laughs as apparently I was giving the impression that I wanted my family to surf me down the table!!!! HAHA.

Well it was the right action but wrong occasion and it got me thinking about my secret dream to be crowd surfed to my final resting place.

When we are born into this life we are held in arms and so why not when leaving it loudly with favourite metal music.

Destination would be a moss covered hill in a forest protected for eternity and so I expect I will have to find and buy that forest sometime.

I would like two trees planted nearby and the first being a birch tree as it has become quiet sacred to me now that would keep the second oak tree company till it is grown and then to make sure there is enough fungi to maintain connectivity and health amongst all the trees.

Back at the Fuss! I did take the opportunity to say that my family were the most important thing in my life and I thanked my son Marcus for use of the amex card he lets me borrow when I go on a journey. (just for emergencies)

And I wanted to honour my grandson Toby for doing a PhD (WOW)

And I presented JuJu with the one painting of the Dancing White Goddess that she really liked just in gratitude for the lovely food made with a big heart.

My birthday card from Marcus was like a bingo card with numbers from 16 to 70 with the words.

"Age is just a number Pick One" this put a big smile on my face as not only was it an affectionate cute and clever gesture but it took me right to the memory of when Teemu Mäntysaari wrote a similar thing about me on his fb page.

Mad and Magic indeed.

And the big birthday was a perfect finale to a four year adventure but I think this story does not appear to have an end just many new beginnings.

Honouring MOG and MEG

I want to give a big thank you to my two amazing granddaughters, Morgana and Megan who helped to launch me into a new world of experience and then they became a sort of Guardian Angel base camp on the other end of my mobile. Always ready and willing to give words of comfort in challenging times and wise advise on tricky situations and of course on line ticket buying.

Their constant presence was such a comfort and grounding force for me that it allowed the gentle chaos to emerge and do its thing in an organic way as I think the journey was a lot about what did not happen so creating the right cracks in it for the magic to shine through.

I listened to Megan's request to leave a magic story from Soumenlinna for you then I will just excuse myself for a while cos there are some more Magic stories waiting to be written and I don't want to keep them waiting too long.

In Honour of Wintersun

And there are pockets of sound from both Jari Maenpaa's voice and electric guitar and harmonies from the band that creates the perfect pitch to put shivers in my head a longing in my heart and tears in my eyes. And actually a dance in my soul which some day my earthly feet might just learn to trace the steps to in this world.

 ...and I wonder!

(Here Now You Finish It)

THE TROLL COLLECTIVE

Dora the story teller was paying a nostalgic visit to the first stone that delivered her a story. It was on the far side of Soummenlinna island right next to the sea on a secluded beach and she took the Erkel Derkel Stick with her for inspiration as she was looking for a new story. When she found the first stone she lay down on top of it and placed her head upon it with her face pressed gently against it and she rested an open hand palm down and waited patiently. She looked out onto the ocean where the hot summer sun was setting the sea ablaze with millions of glittering crystal stars and she breathed in this vision for a while, enjoying the gentle sound of the sea. Then from inside the big stone she could hear strange echos almost like a drum roll; very quiet but then getting louder till it positively roared like thunder! Dora instinctively jumped up and back stepped a few paces though not a moment too soon as a line in the stone just ripped open revealing a large chasm. Then six figures emerged, five of whom were very tall, and brandishing weapons like large clubs and iron swords; they had long dark hair that framed very big swarthy faces, two eyes that were wolf like and almost black with an orange glow in the centre and they wore grey and black tunics and leggings with leather footwear that were bound with long lengths of thick twine. Dora mentally added their hands as weapons because they were huge and hairy with great talons and then after feeling quiet giddy from the stench that emanated freely from them, she added this as another weapon. They growled and ground their teeth and made strange noises in their throats which Dora found quiet terrifying but she remembered that talking could buy time and as they had not eaten her yet she tried it; so in a voice she hoped would not betray the fear she felt she said "Greetings other worldly visitors and welcome to our Earth Realm, I am Dora the story teller." The biggest creature addressed her using some very deep growls and then Dora was saved by the sixth figure who was a tall cloaked female of unclear origin and when she let down her hood Dora saw that she had very long shiny black hair that framed a strange but handsome face and her posture was firm but graceful as she faced Dora with a gaze from two deep grey and violet eyes and spoke thus. "I am Dagda of The Drollek and the one addressing you is Captain Drog of the Noble Troll Collective, he is thanking you for opening the Dimensional Portal and I would not disagree with him on that point as he then says that because of it he will not eat you as you are obviously a Wizard." Dagda spoke softer to Dora now as she confided that Trolls are very wary of Wizards and will avoid them if they can; then she said she would make a spell to enable Dora to understand Troll Speak and with a slight wave of her hand across Dora s throat and some quietly uttered words she proclaimed the spell complete. Then Dora could understand the Troll captain say "We are on orders to collect the Princess from the mighty Giant King Bolderan as payment agreed for our services in the great Giant wars. Dora froze on the spot, "GIANTS!? How can that be ? Surely they belong in human legend in our ancient past" so she said this rather anxiously "Er yes I see um, would you be so kind as to remind me when that was exactly" Dagda spoke in answer saying "You are a young Wizard and could be forgiven for not remembering the great giant wars as it was just after the Ice Giants arrived" Dora felt quiet lost now and was struggling to find the words but she remembered that Erkel had told her to whisper his name if she needed help and then to listen to the quiet voice for the reply, and so she did as quietly as possible, she breathed his name and added help! Erkel answered immediately saying "All is well, the Trolls just had a wrong spell and have gone off their time line" "Thank you Elf" breathed Dora feeling confidant now about how to proceed. So she addressed the main Troll thus "Captain Drog may one ask which spell you relied on to cross from your dimension to the human realm as I believe there is a small time difference" Well you could have heard a pin drop in the silence that followed as all of the Trolls jaws collectively dropped leaving their mouths wide open to release rather a lot of putrid slime that dripped down over their chins to the ground. (Trolls smell perfectly sweet when in their own forest but leaving them makes them very anxious and that creates a strange chemical reaction which produces a putrid odour.) Then came guilty looks from one Troll to another until all eyes rested on Sargeant Snerk. Captain Drog roared "Well Sargeant Snerk l believe the task of employing a wizard for the job fell to you; indeed l distinctly heard you insist that you knew a most respected Wizard right for the job." Dora covered her ears as the earth literally shook at the Troll's next roar. "Well what do you have to say for yourself" Snerk looked quiet helpless as lots of putrid sweat beads gathered on his forehead and dripped down his sorry looking face and he just sort of gibbered some confused babble. "Well" roared Captain Drog again "Dragon got your tongue" He then pulled himself up to an impressive hight and towered over Snerk as he said "I will tell you what happened; you said you,d sort it and funds were delivered to you to ensure the getting of a good Wizard for the travelling spell and you did what you always do and drank away most of the funds on Troll nectar, panicked and ended up with some charlatan, am I right Sargeant Snerk?" He bellowed so loud that the sea actually shook a little. Snerk just crumpled and looked pleadingly up at the Captain which Dora thought was quiet surreal and added the roar as another weapon. It does not matter if the Troll Captain Drog was right or wrong because in the Troll laws, as long as there is some kind of explanation then justice is served and he did seam quiet pleased with his summary of the situation and said "You see that's why I'm in charge because I have insight". The Troll soldiers wanted very much at this point to please their Captain that they all shouted "Hurrah" and clapped madly for a while, which nearly sent Dora flying from the air currant disturbance. Any how Drog seemed very pleased now and then said "The problem is we need a Princess and we don t have one, solution is we just go and get any female to take back to our King, job done any questions?. Dagda then said she had a magic amulet that would take them to the perfect Princess. Captain Drog was keen to agree to any thing that would get the job done and send him back home so he said yes to that. Troll soldier Drib was feeling anxious, he missed the great dark forests of his Troll Realm that were his home. It is said that Trolls are a mixture of Earth, Tree and Stone, indeed this would seem to be so as most of their friends are stones which they can become quiet attached to. Some of these stones are actually quiet creature like in appearance eg: frozen Troll Stones that look as if they would come to life and move about. And great elephant shapes or smaller perfectly round stones that are half covered with moss and look as if they re about to speak. He was remembering the smells of his forest home; the scent of the pine trees and the small needle leaves that made a fine tea. The mossy earth had a different scent depending on the time of day. At dawn there was a damp mist scent and at midday it was tinged with wood smoke; by evening all the smells of the forest joined in a rich aromatic scent. There were the gigantic ancient evergreen trees that also were counted amongst their close friends so there was a lot to miss and he longed to be back in his Troll cave, sitting by a great log fire, breathing in all the smells of the forest and watching the shadows on the cave wall at night; and then it dawned on him. THERE WERE NO SHADOWS IN THIS PLACE !!!!! He was very upset to realise this and wailed to the captain. "We don't got no shadows! and me and Blod and Dred we likes to cast great big shadows when we is on a hunting raid cos it do make us look very fierce and powerful; how can we look fierce without shadows." Dagda spoke up again saying "I can make a small shadow spell, we are in the land of the Midnight Sun and its the Night of Endless Day and so there are no shadows here." It was agreed, so Dagda made a slight movement with her hand and whispered a spell word and then five big shadows appeared and attached to each Troll. Dora was most intrigued with Dagda's use of Magic and wondered what else may be revealed about her like her place of origin because she had Wizard Ways yet looked so very not Wizard but her thoughts were interrupted now by another sound of thunder as a yet another figure appeared at the Dimensional doorway on the big stone. He looked quiet green and plump and frog like but wearing a gold crown, with a blue silk suit with silk lace ruffles on his silk white shirt and shiny purple shoes. Dora was reminded of the tale of the Frog Prince when,he spoke "Ah greetings fair maidens and gentlemen" as he bowed low. "I am Gremek, known as the Frog Prince, I trust you are familier with the story! And now would some one be so kind as to tell me which Realm this is?" Dagda answered saying "This is the Human Realm" and she explained the mission to him.

"Aha, so there is a Princess involved" said the Frog Prince approvingly. "Well that is marvellous and l have a way of detecting if she be a real Princess as when she kindly consents to plant a little kiss on my cheek then my appearance will alter noticeably." Dora was bursting to ask all sorts of important questions of this strange green creature and began with "Excuse me your Highness but don't you belong in a child's Faery Tale story?" Dagda interceded at once saying "We have no time to speak of this now but later you may ask your questions" Every time the strange female spoke intrigued Dora "And the intrigue was certainly piling up"she thought. Dagda said to the Troll Captain that they should take Dora because Wizards can be useful and also the Frog creature as he will ensure them taking a real Princess which was agreed and the company started out in the direction that she chose. The Troll shadows were all in place and at least twice the size of each of their hosts and were towering as requested and looked most impressive. They walked with stealth as ordered by their Captain, so the Troll Collective all hunched up their shoulders and moved their eyes from side to side but the shadows seemed to have a problem with this new stance and became just a little bit out of alignment which made the Trolls hop and step a bit in order to keep up! Dora tried not to laugh but it was the funniest thing she had ever seen so she held her mouth with her hand in order to muffle any escaping giggles. The Frog Prince Gremek looked perfectly at ease with this drama and walked majestically behind Dagda who was surging ahead. Then they came to a full stop just outside a big stone granite building with a big door and Dagda suggested that Drib and Blod keep guard on the outside door. Dora was feeling very anxious about the reality of any human being confronted by these very large smelly Trolls who were brandishing weapons so she quickly said that she would knock the door and then she did just three times. Footsteps were heard shortly after and a woman with a face mask on and hair bunched up very high in rollers holding a mobile phone with one hand which she was talking loudly on mobile and a pot of goo in the other, opened it. This sight was not new to Dora but the Trolls cringed and shuddered at this "Demonic creature" as Sargeant Snerk would call her later when recounting the tale. This was Dorcas Doolally who is the aunt of Deidra Doolally, sister of Dennis Doolally, sister in law to Dweena Doolally and daughter of grandma Edna Doolally. When Dorcas saw the company on the door step she just called out "Dede its for you hoo!" and then walked away still talking loudly to a shopping channel. "Yes that's right on holiday for a few weeks, yes I want the singing foot massager" and then she was gone back up the stairs. Dagda made a signal for all the company of Trolls, Froggy type and Dora to enter the house and they followed a music and chat noise that Dora knew was a radio they followed the sound and entered the room causiously. There was a very old lady sitting on an armchair in front of a log fire with a big pot of tea on a small table in front of her and a radio on a shelf next to her. It was a very big room and Grandma Edna Doolally looked very small in it,then she saw the guests and offered a most cheery "Hello dearies how nice of you to visit me l,ve just made a nice pot of tea so if you seat yourselves we can all have a cup"! She enlisted the help of Dora to help pour the drink as she said her eyesight was not too good and asked everyone to speak up as she was hard of hearing also. Dora, Dagda and Frog Prince sat opposite on a comfy sofa whilst Dred, Snerk and the Captain Drog remained standing. When tea was poured it was offered all round and Captain Drog held his tiny cup in the palm of his huge hand and threw the contents into his huge open mouth and with one gulp it was gone he then carefully offered back the cup and his men having watched the process followed suit. Then Dagda said to Edna"We have come looking for the Princess is she here?" Grandma heard the word Princess and said "Oh yes our Princess she's drying her nails cos it's her eighteenth birthday today and she's off to a music concert but I expect she will be down soon" Dred muttered something about treasure and disappeared up stairs and followed the echo of voices. In one room Dweena Doolally was watching her favourite soap opera on a large tv because even on holiday she liked to keep up with it. She was quiet a large woman and hopelessly addicted to the Crunchy Lady Snacks which she always kept next to her side on a small table but were always on the way to being devoured indeed there was hardly a break in between bites and all conversations had to occur above a mouth stuffed full of crunchy things. Dred checked that his shadow was well represented and entered the room; he did not know what manner of creature he encountered but he thought for sure it was a Wizard as it had a Magic Eye Box where many events were unfolding in the future and he greatly desired to have this treasure. His desire for it overcame his fear and he made a sudden dash for it, unfortunately for him it was right at the crucial point in the soap that Dweena was watching and everyone in the Doolally house hold knows two things; which is, DO NOT interrupt her when she s watching her favourite tv programme and secondly DO NOT get in the way of herself and the tv EVER! Dred did both and Dweena, s reaction was immediate as she flung a can of fizzy pop straight at his head and caught him right between the eyes which was accompanied by a huge shriek! DRED, FLED! Out the door and down the stairs to safety beside his Troll Captain where he quietly nursed his poor wounded head. Snerk did not fare any better for he had gone to dad Dennis, s room seeking treasure being careful to align with his huge shadow first and dad was watching the world cup football match, Dora knew that because every so often there was a shout of GOAL or just a shout for a not goal. Any how Trolls don't know this game and Snerk same as Dred thought this was a Wizard with a Magic Eye and he just had to have it so he made a grab for it and got a smack from dad, s very fast beer can right between the eyes for his trouble, accompanied by a huge roar that could rival Captain Drog! Snerk fell on his shadow and went sailing down the stairs at great speed and sailed right out the open front door to land on top of Drib and Blod and that is where he stayed. Blod and Drib had gotten hold of a big box of Crunchy Lady Snacks and were gobbling them up fast, so Snerk joined in and pretty soon forgot about anything else. In Grandma's room Deidra now appeared blowing on her nails and looking very lovely with her long black and red hair which perfectly complimented her black lipstick. She was wearing a black and red lace dress with big black boots and Dagda addressed her saying "We are looking for a Princess to which Dede replyed "Yes that's me are you all going to the gig too?" Dede is used to seeing strange looking festival crowds so to her these Trolls all looked normal. Dora stepped in now saying "No not exactly but these interesting looking folk would like to invite you to an adventure of a life time" Dora could not think of any thing else to say and now felt rather foolish but Dagda nodded her approval and then Gremek stepped forward and offered a small golden ball to Dede saying "This is a gift for a Princess and all I ask in return is a small kiss on the cheek" Dede looked enchanted and accepted the gold ball and then gave him a gentle peck on his cheek which took immediate effect and the Frog Prince transformed from a rather round frog to a tall and handsome Prince. Captain Drog took that as the signal to act and now stepped in saying "We are the Troll Collective and we have come to take you to the Troll king" Dede did understand Troll Speak, as years of listening to her mother talk with her mouth full of crunchy snacks sounded similar so she said "Oh is that a new metal band? Anyway you,ll have to wait till my nails dry first" Captain Drog was just about to grab her when his shadow began to misbehave and started swaying against the wall in time to a tango playing on the radio and then Dred's shadow did likewise much to the amusement of Dede and then the two shadows became partners and were dancing quiet beautifully and Edna who forgot that she didn't have a tv exclaimed "Oh look its strictly come dancing! Oooh don't they look lovely" Drog did the only thing an embarrassed Troll could do and made a Troll binding spell saying "We are Troll and we are taking you to our King in our Troll Realm" Dede was lifted slightly and guided toward the door and then her mobile rang it was her friend Tracy "Hi Tracy" said Dede "No I'm wearing red and black lace an leather so don't wear pink cos we'll clash" and right now I am being crowd surfed out of my door. (crowd surfing happens at metal music festivals where willing people are lifted above the festival goers and handed from one pair of hands to another until they reach the front of the stage where they are gently caught hold of and released on the ground) But just before anything else occurred Captain Drog sneezed a little and some putrid slime shot right onto Dede's lovely dress! Well now, there is a particular noise that girls make when they find a spider on their clothes which is a kind of Ooooer! And that was not it. And then there is a noise that girls make when their nail polish gets smudged which is a kind of OOOHHH! But that was not it either. For the noise that Dede made was so fierce that they still talk about it in the Troll Realm to this day because it broke the binding spell completely and then this very annoyed girl planted a great big punch on Captain Drog's nose and actually sent him flying right across the garden to land in a heap on top of Drib, Blod and Snerk. Then Dede screamed "Look what you've done to my dress!" Dora grabbed a towel from the house and cleaned it off best as she could then Dagda made a small cleaning spell and the dress was as good as new then they turned to see Captain Drog nurse a hurt nose and eating the crunchy lady snacks that had been apprehended. Then some thing happened to all the Trolls as they just seemed to lose their wits after eating the crunchy snacks and they just sat on the ground as if nothing else mattered apart from eating snacks. Stranger even still were the Trolls Shadows that were becoming quiet third dimensional and eating the snacks also!. Dagda said that she had borrowed the shadows from a Shadow Realm and had to send them back before they became fully third dimensional and ran out of control! So she instantly rushed inside to Grandma's room where Drog's shadow was now sitting on the couch with Snerk's shadow and were being given endless cups of tea by Grandma and eating the Lady Crunchy Snacks. Dagda said a quick spell and they vanished. "Leaving already are you? see you again, do pop in the doors always open". said Grandma. The outside shadows were quickly dispatched also and then Dagda beckoned to Dora, Dede and Gremek to follow her as she led them to the little sandy beach and then said "So here we all are, good! and now l will explain" and she drew out from her cloak a Pink Crystal Ball and said that it was a Timeless Moment Memory Crystal from her Faery Realm and that there are many of these stored away in the Timeless Garden and when Elementals travel they usually take one or two for comfort and she bade Dede to gaze into it which the girl did and then she gasped "Oooh that's me as a small child when I was visiting Santa Clause in the Arctic Circle" Dagda asked her if she remembered what she wished for but Dede only had a vague memory of it so Dagda carefully took out a piece of paper with scribbles on and a child's drawing of a Frog Prince. "Well this is your note to Santa Clause asking for your wish to be granted which was to kiss the Frog Prince and then go with him to Faery land" Dagda paused for a while to enable Dede to digest all the information and then continued saying "I am a Walker of Worlds and I visit the Earth Realm regularly, on this occasion I was helping Santa Clause when you came along Dierdra and after I heard your wish to Santa Clause my heart melted toward you and I was determined to help you have your wish come true. So I found out where you lived and then enlisted the help of my good friend Gremek who also is a Walker of Worlds also and after showing him the memory in the crystal his heart melted toward you also" Gremek took up the story now and he took out another pink crystal from his waistcoat pocket and bade Deirdra gaze in it also which she did. Then she cupped her face in both her hands as she saw herself as three years of age sitting next to a Froggy looking Prince with a gold crown and blue silk clothes; he looked quiet green and she had tight red curly hair and a big smile on her lovely little face. She and her companion were sitting on the same rock as this day.

Dede looked up at Gremek and said "That is me and that is you" and two tears fell from her eyes as she was beginning now to remember her invisible friend. "Yes" said Gremek "I was your invisible friend and I wove a spell so that only you could see me" Dede was beginning to remember now "We had so much fun and I was not alone any more and we had adventures in Faeryland" Gremek replied, "Yes that is so and we always went by night so that you would not be missed and in the morning if you wanted to talk about them it would seem like a dream to the human folk" "I kept a diary" said the girl "And I still have it in my magic box but as I grew older it was difficult to read the scribbles after you went away; Why did you go away" Dede now looked sadly into Gremek's eyes, so he gently took her hand and said "You were growing up and I had to let you make human friends for a while in order for you to grow in this world and make your own choices, but I did not go far and I always kept an eye on you and now you are of age today and so you can choose what life you want; I promised you a life in my Faery Realm and today if you wish it still then I will gladly take you there with all my heart" Then Dagda spoke saying these words. "The Trolls were on a mission to find a Princess and as the time was right I and Gremek hitched a ride on their Magic Travel Spell, being careful to add our own guidance to this place and of course I would not let the Trolls hurt you but I am greatly impressed by your fighting spirit for this shows greatness". She continued. If you decide to go with Gremek I will remain so that your family will not fret at your loss and I will make a spell so that they will see only you when they look upon me" Dede had a lot to think about but she made her decision in three minutes and said "I have waited all my life for this moment and I cannot miss this adventure now and I am remembering so much now that I cannot wait to go and see all my friends in your Faery Realms again like we used to" Gremek was very happy and said "Yes they all remember you with love as you took your own magic there and they will be glad to have your company once again" "Oh do they have wifi?" asked Dede and Gremek replied saying "No but we have Magic Mirrors and all manner of Natural Magic that I am sure will delight you" Dede offered her concert tickets to Dagda saying "If you are going to be me then this is the music that I love, they,re a local band called Wintersun" Dagda accepted graciously and suggested that as it was Deidra's special birthday they all go to the concert, then she gave Dede a Magic Amulet to take her safely from one Realm to another. So Dede, Dagda, Gremek and Dora all went to the metal music concert which they all enjoyed tremendously. And they all took turns to be crowd surfed. Then at the end of the day, it was time for Dede and Gremek to leave for his Faery Realm. "I do hope we can meet again as I would love to write your story" said Dora to Dede who smiled and replied that maybe one day Dora might visit her in the Faery Realm, then with some fare thee wells they were gone back through the portal on the beach. Dagda and Dora returned to the Trolls who had been munching snacks all day long and then Dagda made a spell which brought the Trolls back to their senses and addressed them saying. "The Troll King is noble enough but very old now and he has already so many Princesses that he has forgotten most of them". (Captain Drog remembered well that the Troll Kings land was awash with beautiful princesses and they each had to have their own castle and fine clothes and servants which was very costly. Then he only saw them once a year at his birthday feast where he would try to count them all which was exhausting and so he always ended up falling asleep on his Troll throne) "What would be more useful to him are the Crunchy Snacks that steal away the wits of all who eat them" continued Dagda "And Captain Drog could say that the Giant King very reluctantly parted with them as they were his greatest treasure and then of course there will be great honour's heaped upon all the Troll Collective and promotions". The Trolls good spirits all returned after this pep talk and collecting more snacks they departed for their Realm. Dora then asked Dagda if she knew Erkel Derkel to which she replied "Yes l do, he is known amongst my Tribe as Erkel of the Derkel and I am honoured to have had his friendship for ages now; we meet sometimes in the Elf Collective" Dora smiled also and said "Of course and it all makes sense now because there's always some magic happening when he is about" They both talked freely now about the Elf Collective and the great journey with the Baby Pine Cones and then how Dora met the floating branch. Then Dagda shared this with Dora saying "There are many Stories with their origins in very ancient times when Magic ruled all the Realms and to catch and weave them into this world now is important work". Dora recalled Erkels words about all the Realms uniting and it did give her much pause for thought. Then Dora and Dagda said fare thee well for now and promised to keep connected in the Human Realm. A while after going to the metal music concert, Dagda told Dora she liked it so much that she formed her own Metal Music Band and named it Troll Maiden. She became popular very fast and her singing voice (it was said by all who heard it) could put everyone in a Magic Trance State!. Deirdra reclaimed her beautiful magic life in Gremek's Faery Realm and dressed like a proper Princess now in gorgeous silk, satin and velvet dresses. She was welcomed by all the strange Magic friends of her childhood and they made her feel like she had never left Faery land. Dora looked forward to writing her story. Erkel Derkel continued to provide Magic and stories for Dora. The Troll Captain Drog became quiet famous and was promoted to General and enjoyed telling his version of the story! You know the one where the Great Giant King Bolderan reluctantly gave up his greatest treasure, the Crunchy Snacks that could steal any Creature, s wits who dared to eat one? Well they are now under lock and key in the deepest cave in the tallest mountain, guarded by a small army of Troll Soldiers. Sargeant Snerk was promoted to Captain and did tell a very good story of the adventure where he was the Hero, but Trolls love a good story so they didn't question his version too deeply. Drib, Dred and Blod returned to their fire lit caves in the Ancient Dark Forest where they lived happily with their friends, the Stones and the Trees...

www.ingramcontent.com/pod-product-compliance
Lightning Source LLC
Chambersburg PA
CBHW060525100426
42743CB00009B/1434